THE MEANING OF THE MEXICAN REVOLUTION

PROBLEMS IN LATIN AMERICAN CIVILIZATION

UNDER THE EDITORIAL DIRECTION OF
EDWIN LIEUWEN, UNIVERSITY OF NEW MEXICO

INDIAN LABOR IN THE SPANISH INDIES — Was There Another Solution? — *Edited by John Francis Bannon, S.J., Saint Louis University*

THE BOURBON REFORMERS AND SPANISH CIVILIZATION — Builders or Destroyers? — *Edited by Troy S. Floyd, University of New Mexico*

THE MEANING OF THE MEXICAN REVOLUTION — *Edited by Charles C. Cumberland, Michigan State University*

Other volumes in preparation

PROBLEMS IN LATIN AMERICAN CIVILIZATION

THE MEANING OF
THE MEXICAN REVOLUTION

EDITED WITH AN INTRODUCTION BY

Charles C. Cumberland, MICHIGAN STATE UNIVERSITY

D. C. HEATH AND COMPANY
Lexington, Massachusetts

6627

Table of Contents

THE PHILOSOPHY OF THE REVOLUTION

LUIS CABRERA
The Revolution Is Constructive   1

NICOLÁS CANO
The Revolution Was Fought to Equalize Capital and Labor   4

ALVARO OBREGÓN
The Revolution Was Fought for Democracy   9

JORGE VERA ESTAÑOL
The Revolution Has Been Destructive   15

THE CHURCH-STATE CONFLICT

ARTURO M. ELÍAS
The Church Has Exploited the People   21

BISHOP PASCUAL DÍAZ
The Policy of the Government Is Anti-Religious   24

JAMES CANNON, JR.
The Church Has Suppressed Religious Liberties   28

WILLIAM FRANKLIN SANDS
Mexico Is a Godless State   32

AGRARIAN REFORM

W. W. CUMBERLAND
Agrarian Reform Is Prolonging Poverty   36

RAMÓN BETETA
Agrarian Reform Is Beneficial   41

CLARENCE SENIOR
Agrarian Reform Has Brought Democracy and Increased
Production   47

ECONOMIC NATIONALISM: OIL EXPROPRIATION

ROSCOE B. GAITHER
The Illegality of the Expropriations   57

MEXICAN GOVERNMENT
The Expropriations Were Legal and Necessary   61

HARLOW S. PERSON
A Historic, Irrepressible Conflict   67

ECONOMIC POLICY: INDUSTRIALIZATION

SANFORD A. MOSK
Industrialization Is Possible   73

FRANK TANNENBAUM
Industrialization Will Be a Calamity   78

MANUEL GERMÁN PARRA
Mexico Must and Will Industrialize   83

POLITICS: THE DEMOCRATIC PROCESS

A. SILVA VILLALOBOS
The Need for Civic Education   90

MANUEL GÓMEZ MORÍN
Democracy Does Not Exist in Mexico   94

ROBERT E. SCOTT
Mexico's Democratic Syndrome   99

Suggestions for Additional Reading   107

Introduction

THE Mexican will tell you that Mexico has suffered many revolutions but only one Mexican Revolution; written in this fashion the words refer to that vast and bloody upheaval which began in 1910. This revolution, with its intermittent warfare lasting for more than ten yars, cost the Mexicans dearly in both human and material losses: possibly a million dead and a billion dollars in damages. In one way or another the Revolution touched, intimately, all Mexicans, save those indigenes who lived in extreme isolation. Violence became a way of life, either something to take part in or to flee from. Under these circumstances, the Revolution, in upper case, engendered violent emotions on the part of those who experienced it.

Mexicans agree that a revolution has taken place, but they do not agree among themselves on the meaning of the Revolution. Each has his own interpretation of the movement's philosophy, the course of developments, and the terminal date. The official party, and, accordingly, the public officials holding office under its aegis, contend that the Revolution remains an integral part of Mexican life, vital and viable to this day; government policy is still consistently justified in terms of the Revolution. The late José Vasconcelos and many who agree with him, on the other hand, insist that the true Revolution died even before Carranza met his death in 1920 and that Alvaro Obregón buried it in the succeeding four years. Others hold that the true Revolution reached its peak under Lázaro Cárdenas (1934–40), or Manuel Avila Camacho (1940–46), or Miguel Alemán (1946–52). Some of these feel that the more recent administrations have been guilty of the grossest perversion, of destroying the ideals of the Revolution in the name of the Revolution.

This welter of confusion stems from the lack of *a* revolutionary philosophy or philosophic system, and from the multiplicity of contending concepts and their adherents. One high official in an opposition party, not particularly sympathetic with the revolutionary trend, insists that a basic philosophy of the Revolution "does not exist"; in one way he is correct. During the epic phase of the movement, each regional chieftain, through his pronouncements or his policies, gave some indication of his own ultimate aims and, therefore, added to the body of thought concerning the purpose of the Revolution. Occasionally those aims were clearly enunciated, as was the case with Emiliano Zapata; but more often they were nebulous and open to a variety of interpretations. Each Mexican, then, has selected those statements which most clearly accord with his own concepts and has given those statements an interpretation he believes to be the true one. To some, the *real* cause of the revolution was the antiquated land system, with all its injustices and inefficiencies; to these men the purpose of the movement was land reform, and nothing more. They who so contend can find ample evidence to support their position in the statements of Francisco Madero, Zapata, Carranza, Obregón, and a multitude of others. But even here there is little agreement, for one man sees agrarian reform in terms of communal land ownership, another sees it as small private holdings, and still another views it in terms of efficient agricultural production — and each seeks, and finds, public statements by revolutionary heroes to support his views. To a number of those who fought, the Revolution's principal cause was labor injustice and its aim, therefore, an amelioration of the workingman's plight through proper labor-management relations. But what are these proper relations, and what role should government play in them? To others the revolution meant little more than changing the political system, the end of the dictatorship, and the inauguration of a representative government implying, in and of itself, nothing in social or economic change. The quarrel over causes, aims and ends had begun even before Madero's military movement; time has dimmed the ferocity but not the bitterness of the contending points of view.

The first group of selections presented here demonstrates in part these opposing views but certainly does not cover them all. Luis Cabrera, speaking before the American Academy of Political and Social Science in 1917, couched the revolutionary aims in vague terms of human liberty and human welfare. The social system demanded destruction, he said, so that a decent society could be developed through a process of reconstruction. Nicolás Cano, a laboring man of little education but great confidence in the decency and power of his class, wanted from the revolution only an opportunity for organized labor to work out a solution with management, free from the trammels of government; far from demanding government support for labor, he insisted only on government permission to strike. Alvaro Obregón's political manifesto herein included emphasized only the political aspect of the revolutionary program. His career both before and after he wrote this rationale for becoming a candidate in 1920 strongly indicates that his concept of the revolution was indeed much deeper than that of mere political change, but the fact that he saw fit to make his plea in political terms suggests that a great number of people so saw it. Jorge Vera Estañol, writing from the vantage point of 1957 about events in which he had participated — but not as a member of the revolutionary family — made a distinction between the Revolution and the governments which have followed. The Revolution, he averred, ended with the drafting of the Constitution of 1917, and the succeeding

governments have made a great show of talking about the Revolution but have failed completely to fulfill any of the promises incorporated into that document. His view was diametrically opposed to that of Cabrera's; Estañol insisted that the revolution in Mexico was not only unnecessary but destroyed an evolutionary process which, had it been allowed to continue, would have made of Mexico a great nation long since.

Regardless of Madero's original aims, or Carranza's, or Villa's, or Zapata's, the Mexican Revolution has developed along a fairly well-defined but complex course, and an examination of that course is essential to a comprehension of the Revolution's meaning. The trend has been definitely, and at times violently, anticlerical. Agrarian reform, or at least a changing relationship between man and land (whether this change has constituted "reform" is the subject of hot debate) has been a consistent feature. A militant nationalism, shown in a variety of ways and highlighted by the 1938 oil expropriation, has perhaps been the characteristic most obvious to the citizen of the United States. Government intervention into the economic process, be it direct ownership of such essential resources as hydroelectric power or petroleum, or the more circuitous policy of exchange controls and monetary devaluation, has been patent since 1910 and particularly marked in the last thirty years. Finally, the Mexican political process has passed through a series of stages which make of the 1966 political system something quite different from that existing prior to 1910. The remaining selections of this booklet deal with these five facets of revolutionary development although there are others (particularly education and labor) which have been of great significance.

Church-State relations, always troubled and sometimes vicious, have caused grave concern to Mexican and foreigner alike. The issue has been — and is — simply stated by the revolutionary governments: assigning to organized religion in general, and to the Roman Catholic Church in particular, a proper role in Mexican society. The difficulty between clerical and anticlerical, between Church and State, began with independence and became endemic during the nineteenth century. Occasionally open violence flared, as during the so-called War of Reform (1858–1861); but even during periods of quiescence such as that in the Díaz regime, the animosity remained barely hidden below the surface. The military movements after 1910 gave the anticlericals ample opportunity to vent their spleens. Revolutionists sacked churches, shot priests, exiled nuns and then wrote into the Constitution of 1917 a series of articles which closely circumscribed the actions of the Church as an institution and of clerics as her agents. They were convinced, as a delegate to the Constitutional Congress expressed it, that "the Clergy appears as the cruelest and most tenacious enemy of our liberties." But members of the clergy and their friends, the proclericals, could scarce conceive of themselves as villains, and they fought back as best they could. The late 1920's saw a high point of inflammation with the Cristero rebellion. For nearly three years rebels battled government forces while shouting "Long Live Christ the King," and the clergy refused to perform the rites of the Church. Three of the four selections included were written during the clash and represent varying shades of opinion. The fourth, written by a thoughtful U.S. Catholic statesman, was written at a slightly later time when another serious struggle seemed imminent.

Mexican Consul General Arturo Elías, in a small book written to convince the U.S. public of the righteousness of his government's position, drew a sharp distinction between Catholic dogma and clerical action, between religion as a belief system and the Church as a social institution. The clergy — and especially the Episcopate — he argued, was concerned solely with the retention of clerical, economic, political, and social power, and stooped to

any level to guarantee that power. In the brief extracts taken from his book for this volume, Elías is concerned with the anticlerical provisions of the Constitution of 1857 which, he said, were fully justified since the clergy had made a mockery of Catholicism and the Church had destroyed the virtues of Christ. But Bishop Pascual Díaz of Tabasco, exiled by President Calles and addressing himself to a U.S. audience from San Antonio, Texas, insisted that the issue was between two contrary philosophies. The government, he averred, subscribed to the philosophy that all rights of individuals or groups derive from the State and may be curbed or revoked by the State; the Church, on the other hand, subscribed to the philosophy of inherent rights much as that philosophy is expressed in the U.S. Declaration of Independence. He closed his argument by reiterating a statement widely circulated by clerical sympathizers: the government attacked not solely the clergy, nor even alone the Catholic Church; it attacked religion itself. Methodist James Cannon, Jr., saw the issue as one of real religious freedom, but from the opposite side of the fence from Díaz. Cannon, exhibiting a strain of anti-Catholicism, sympathized not at all with the Catholic Episcopate's argument that government action threatened religious freedom; quite the contrary, he saw these actions as the only hope for ultimate religious freedom in Mexico. The anticlerical campaign, he said, was fully justified. Finally, William Franklin Sands, an eminent Catholic layman with wide journalistic and diplomatic experience, decided after a lengthy investigation in Mexico that the government policy was destructive to religious freedom and to religion itself.

Since 1935, when Sands wrote, the legal situation of the Church has changed only slightly, although in practice the state intervenes very little in religious affairs. But the questions remain, as do the suspicions. Has the Church historically been the tool (or even the leader) of the reaction, violently opposed to reform or economic change? Even if this be so, has the harshness of the anticlerical laws and actions been justified? Did the revolutionists, acting through the government, attack the Church, or Catholicism, or organized religion itself?

Land reform remains the sacred cow of the Mexican Revolution, not subject to criticism by anyone aspiring to political prominence. One of the factors contributing to Calles' decline as a political power was his public questioning of the validity of land reform. Every public official must at least pay lip service to the general philosophy of land distribution. But with all this, a serious question remains. Virtually all Mexicans agree that the system prior to the revolution left much to be desired; the hacienda system was inefficient economically and deadening socially. The situation, economic and social, demanded some kind of change, but whether the restoration of the ejido, with its quasicommunal implications and its abandonment of managerial skills, has proved to be the proper vehicle is open to debate. The quarrel has many facets, the most important of which concern agricultural productivity under the ejidal system, the merits of the collectively worked in contrast to the individually worked ejidal plots, the social values of the ejido system, and the relative merits of the ejido and the privately owned farms. The ejido-oriented Mexican will point out that agricultural production has indeed gone up (corn production, for example, has more than tripled since 1910), but the skeptic answers that agricultural production has increased less than the population. The ejidal supporter insists that agrarian reform has brought new dignity and social consciousness to the peasant; the opposition counters that the peasant now has a government instead of an individual as a master. Has the Mexican peasant, in fact, merely exchanged landlords, replacing a sometimes harsh, sometimes kindly, but always intensely human overlord with a cold and dehumanizing bureaucracy? Some of these issues are touched upon in the selections

following. W. W. Cumberland, who shows his bias in his unsolicited strictures on the New Deal, could see nothing but disaster confronting Mexico as a consequence of the ejidal program. Ramó Beteta, one of the architects of Mexico's economic legislation, on the other hand, was convinced that only through a change in the social system could the Mexican peasant gain material well-being. The agrarian reform program, he believed, did in fact augur well for both developments. Clarence Senior, in the excerpt here, was primarily concerned with the development of democratic institutions in a region generally collectivized; in passing he also examined certain aspects of comparative productivity.

On March 18, 1938, President Lázaro Cárdenas, by executive decree, nationalized the major portion of the Mexican oil industry, and in so doing brought an end to one phase of a long-standing controversy and opened another which proved even more bitter. The Constitution of 1917 granted to the Mexican nation ownership of the subsoil deposits and, therefore, directly impinged upon the interests of the oil companies, almost all of which were foreign owned. The companies bitterly contested the principle involved and, by utilizing legal, diplomatic and propagandistic pressures, made every effort to prevent its application. They argued that the Díaz government had granted them legal rights to the subsoil deposits, and that the constitutional provision deprived them of those rights. Furthermore, they contended, the constitution itself forbade retroactivity, and, therefore, both by political theory and by constitutional dictum the subsoil was the property of the companies holding title to the land, and not the property of the nation. The companies viewed every tax or regulatory measure adopted by the government to be nothing more than a thinly veiled attempt to divest them of their properties. The Mexican government, on the other hand, took the position that the Díaz concessions to the oil companies had constituted a destruction of a hallowed and consistent principle dating from pre-Conquest Spain and that, therefore, the constitutional provisions were a return to a norm violated by Díaz. Furthermore, the government insisted, even if one adopted the companies' contention regarding subsoil ownership, as a sovereign nation Mexico had a perfect right, in law and in theory, to institute regulatory and tax measures — and pointed to United States statute and constitutional law to buttress her case. The issue was volcanic; periods of intense or even violent activity were followed by times of apparent calm, but the threat of eruption remained constant. The situation which brought on the expropriation began in 1936 when labor made a series of demands including wage increases and fringe benefits which the companies viewed as ridiculous and the government viewed as justified. When the companies refused to accept the findings and the orders of the Mexican Supreme Court, Cárdenas signed the nationalization decree. Once the president acted, new issues evolved. The affected oil companies, (the decree did not include all companies) supported by the British and the United States governments, contended that Mexico could not pay the indemnity and that the nationalization amounted to confiscation, which the constitution prohibited. Mexico insisted that she could and would pay, but that until the companies agreed to a realistic basis for settlement, no money would change hands. At this point, the question of subsoil ownership again intruded, the companies insisting that the value of the oil reserve be a part of the settlement and the government contending that compensation would be made only for the physical plant and for the oil captured; the difference was, of course, enormous, amounting to nearly half a billion dollars.

From the voluminous and highly controversial literature on the subject, three drastically edited excerpts have been selected. Roscoe Gaither, a member of a Mexican legal association and an experienced observer of Mexican affairs, presents the oil companies' legal case, but against an assumption that Cárdenas from the beginning of his administration sought "to precipitate a crisis and thus give some semblance of an occasion for the seizure." The Mexican government itself was anxious to allay U.S. fears and presented its legal case to the English reading public in a booklet published in 1940, before the final settlement. To give some balance between the widely contrasting, even contradictory, views of the Mexicans and the companies, a selection by Harlow S. Person has been included. Person, by profession a consultant in business economics and management, at the height of the controversy was asked by an unidentified "executive who desired a brief statement of the Mexican oil problem" to prepare a memorandum on the subject. Person's approach was measured; given the suspicions and the premises on both sides, he concluded, the conflict was inevitable and "irrepressible."

In reviewing Mexican experience over the past fifty years, one is struck by the economic experimentation to which the government has been dedicated. Government planners have accepted as a basic tenet the conviction that the economy can grow only under the stimulus of government planning and effort, that tradition and history are against free economic growth. Those responsible for charting economic development have generally rejected the myth of untold Mexican wealth and have confronted the hard reality of an explosive population (both demographically and psychologically) and a primitive economic structure. Unable, for lack of finance, to attack all economic weak spots with equal vigor, the government policy has tended to be pendulous, oscillating between emphasis on agricultural and industrial change. Obregón and Calles, while not neglecting the agrarian sector, put greater emphasis on organized labor, communications, and fiscal systems than on land reform. Cárdenas swung to the opposite extreme and devoted himself almost exclusively to the agricultural scene, except for his fight with the oil companies. Avila Camacho, partly stimulated by demands emanating from World War II, and in part convinced that land distribution itself would never create a healthy economy, moved toward encouraging the industrial sector. His successor, Miguel Alemán, heightened the pace and almost ignored agriculture save for the benefits which would accidentally accrue to that activity as a consequence of impounding water to be used for power and, incidentally, irrigation. While completing the works begun by Alemán, Ruíz Cortines shifted toward agricultural change but emphasized technology and efficiency more than land distribution. López Mateos tended to emphasize industry.

In these shifts, government policy makers have used a great variety of techniques. The government has successively devaluated the peso from the fifty cents U.S. it occupied in 1910, to the eight cents it has commanded since 1954, with each devaluation followed by a significant and rapid rise in prices and a slower rise in wages. Inflation has, therefore, been something of a constant; but it has not been as rampant as in many other countries of Latin America, nor has the nation suffered from a peso black market. On occasion the government has instituted exchange controls, much to the chagrin and inconvenience of a segment of the population, but the more common practice has been to regulate foreign trade through tariffs. Foreign capital has been alternately rejected and wooed, but always closely circumscribed. The government itself has taken on entrepreneurial functions, particularly in the power, fuel, communication, and transportation fields. In addition it has acted as investor-banker in those fields of economic endeavor which, in the minds of government planners, have needed special stimulation. Each of these policies and techniques has been the subject of widespread and sometimes acrimonious debate at home and abroad, but government spokesmen always justify the actions in the name of the Revolution. The

economy has changed enormously in the roughly fifty years since the promulgation of the constitution; in recent years the rate of economic growth has been one of the highest in the world and the economy in general has lost the simplistic character which was so evident in 1910. But some observers insist that the progress has not been progress at all, but retrogression; that the average Mexican citizen has achieved no significant increase in purchasing power since the Díaz regime. Others have concluded that economic change has come at the expense of the Mexican laborer and peasant and that concentration of wealth is more pronounced after fifty years of revolutionary tinkering than it was under Díaz. And many, foreigners and nationals, take the view that economic growth has been less than it would have been had the revolution not occurred.

It is manifestly impossible, in a work of this nature, to examine the multitudinous pro and con arguments concerning economic development over a span of half a century. The selections dealing with the economy have, therefore, been limited to the single question of industrialization, of whether industrial development is a reasonable, or even possible, goal of the Revolution. To debate this issue the editor has selected three outstanding scholars to present their views. Economist Sanford A. Mosk, who made his study shortly after World War II when the nation was just beginning its industrial push, was moderately enthusiastic about the development. He feared that the government was stimulating industry at the expense of other sectors of the economy, that a number of mistakes had been made and that the nation was in for some rough sledding; but in general he was optimistic. Historian Frank Tannenbaum, who has devoted most of his scholarly effort to Latin America and much of it to Mexico, wrote his first book on the Mexican Revolution nearly forty years ago. Since that time he has followed the progress of the revolution with uncommon, almost proprietary, interest. Writing at about the same time as Mosk, he was disappointed that the nation had not developed as rapidly as he had hoped, and he was distraught over the attempts at industrialization. The urge to industrialize, he thought, was a perversion of the original revolution; economically and socially ill-founded. The new economic emphasis would bring ruination, he feared. Mexico, he said, needs a "philosophy of little things," little schools, little dams, little power plants, little lakes, little industries in the form of local crafts using local materials. He was not, he insisted, opposed to an eventual industrialization which he believed to be inevitable. But it was not a part of the original revolutionary program as he interpreted that program, and he felt that the policies then being pursued by the government in the name of the Revolution would bring unnecessary hardship. Mexican economist Manuel Germán Parra was greatly disturbed by Tannenbaum's somber view. In view of Tannenbaum's stature as a scholar, Parra felt called upon to reply to his arguments. Both as a Mexican and as an economist he rejected Tannenbaum's thesis. Mexican industrialization, he said, was not the product solely of government policies; its principal stimulus came from developments in other parts of the world, and nothing the government might have legitimately done would have prevented it. Furthermore, he insisted, it is sheer folly to argue that the agrarian and industrial revolutions may be divorced, since they are mutually dependent and part of the same pattern of improved economic well-being. Without one, the other could not proceed. "The best economic policy will be," he concluded, "that which will promote the greatest and the most rapid material progress which can be translated, in the briefest possible time, into a greater economic independence for the nation and the highest standard of living for the public."

"Effective Suffrage, No Re-election" was the banner under which Madero began his insurrection in late 1910, and the words are a part of every official seal — local, state or national — in Mexico today. Democratic, representative government has been a persistent and daily repeated goal of the Revolution; no Mexican of any political sophistication would dare question the validity of the democratic state. Constitution and law provide for universal suffrage, regular elections place citizens in public office at all levels of government, and a web of regulations concerning campaigning for office have established an institutional framework to guarantee a democracy. But has Mexico arrived at, or even made any progress toward, real political democracy? This question is of significance not only for the evaluation of the Mexican Revolution, for it impinges upon the entire world struggle between the democratic and the antidemocratic systems. To examine this question three excerpts have been selected: one by a somewhat objective Mexican observer, one by a Mexican with a political axe to grind, and one by a United States professor of Political Science.

A. Silva Villalobos, writing in 1958, believed that the revolution had been an almost unqualified success in every sphere save that of politics. He recognized that the constitutional provisions concerning democracy were unrealistic at the time they were written, and did not quarrel with earlier administrations which failed, in fact, to operate within a democratic framework. Furthermore, he argued that, given the traditional culture, any attempt to practice full democracy would have doomed the social revolution to failure. Nevertheless, he insisted, the governments should have been doing something effective to educate the public in democratic ways, and this they had not done. At the time he wrote, he felt that the average Mexican was no more ready to accept the responsibilities of a democratic society than he had been in 1910. "How much time will the Mexican public need to be so ready? An eternity unless the governments of the Revolution decide to initiate the preparation."

Manuel Gómez Morín, the organizer and leading figure in the opposition National Action Party, had lived through ten years of political frustration when he addressed his party's national convention in 1949; if Alemán had any democratic virtues, Gómez Morín could not see them. He was concrete in his charges of pressures, violations of the electoral codes, official party corruption and judicial irresponsibility. He saw the need for some fundamental changes but, unlike Silva Villalobos, he believed that changes in the law would suffice to bring an end to the frauds and to allow true democracy.

Finally, Robert Scott of the University of Illinois gave a measured and dispassionate appraisal of the political system. By 1959, he thought, Mexico had traveled far along the road toward political maturity but had not arrived at a point of democratic perfection. He developed his analysis in terms of what he called a "democratic syndrome"; using sophisticated arguments he concluded: "On the basis of what has taken place since 1910, and especially since 1930, I believe that such a democratic system can be expected to develop in Mexico."

What the Mexican Revolution was, or is, and what effect it has had on Mexican society cannot be answered in easy terms. Change there certainly has been, as these selections clearly demonstrate; but change itself is not necessarily progress. Almost every aspect of Mexican life has been touched by the Revolution, but Mexican life has been influenced as well by an age of incredibly rapid technological change. The selections in this volume do not pretend to show the magnitude of the changes in all walks of life, but they should at least be suggestive.

The Conflict of Opinion

REVOLUTIONARY PHILOSOPHY

"From the slaughter on the battlefields, the mass executions, the plundering in cities, villages, hamlets, and even private houses, there could come only hate, cupidity, and all manner of unhealthy passions; in short, antisocial feelings."

— JORGE VERA ESTAÑOL

"A revolution is not always a source of evil and tears, just as fire does not always produce devastation. . . . In tropical countries . . . the common way of opening fields to cultivation is to clear them with a great fire that consumes indeed much natural wealth, but which at the same time devours rapidly the jungle and, by purifying and fertilizing the soil, saves a large amount of work."

— LUIS CABRERA

CHURCH-STATE RELATIONS

"The Catholic Church is totally incompatible with that kind of state in which religion is abolished or subordinated to the State. That is the kind of State which is beginning to evolve in Mexico. It is of all forms the one that used to be most feared and abhorred by all Americans."

— WILLIAM FRANKLIN SANDS

"The purpose of the Mexican Government has not been and is not today to prevent anyone from preaching or from giving religious instruction to children. It has not attempted to prevent the Church from controlling whatever amount of property is necessary for its *legitimate spiritual* activities."

— JAMES CANNON, JR.

OIL EXPROPRIATION

"All demands possible of acceptance were conceded by the companies. . . . The utterly unreasonable demands, obviously impossible for the companies to meet, were apparently presented with no thought in mind that there might be a compromise. That the whole purpose was to create a crisis is further shown by the result."

— ROSCOE B. GAITHER

"The Standard Oil Company of New Jersey . . . deliberately sought to create the impression . . . that the policy of President Cárdenas' administration was to bring to a head the final realization of a plan conceived by the various governments of Mexico . . . the effect of which was to dispossess the foreign interests . . . by nationalizing their properties. Such an assertion is palpably false. . . ."

— MEXICAN GOVERNMENT

ECONOMIC POLICY

"The city folk . . . would make big plans, procure large foreign funds, organize great industries, discover some magic in 'industrialization,' and have a national economy served by a national market at any cost, even if in their hearts they suspect that it is chiefly a dream, which, because of inadequate resources, cannot be realized. But the ideal of bigness is on them, and they will copy and make plans for the impossible even if the Mexico they love must be sacrificed to their notion of 'progress.'"

— FRANK TANNENBAUM

"History, fortunately, cannot be reversed. Mexico cannot come to be a more rural nation than it now is, nor should it so become. And, on the contrary, even though it perhaps should not become so, Mexico will become an industrial nation. The industrialization process operating among us is not a product of the economic policy followed by the governments of the past but quite the reverse; the economic policy is but a reflection of the industrial revolution which, in turn, is influencing it."

— MANUEL GERMÁN PARRA

POLITICS

"Quite clearly, the rapidly growing number of examples of mass interest about, pressure upon, and participation in, politics, government, and the decision-making process cannot be divorced from the equally compelling increased evidence of presidential policy during both the Ruiz Cortines and the López Mateos administrations of opening the political system to any and every Mexican who becomes sufficiently aware to demand entry to this process."

— ROBERT E. SCOTT

"There has been created, on the foundation of a popular revolution, a circle of political leaders who have put into effect a calculated rotation in public posts and whose number is renewed in a tiny percentage from people well versed in this system which impedes social and political capillarity."

— A. SILVA VILLALOBOS

I. THE PHILOSOPHY OF THE REVOLUTION

The Revolution Is Constructive

LUIS CABRERA

A distinguished and cultured man who was a civilian participant in the early revolutionary process, Luis Cabrera was a long-time advisor to Carranza and a member of his cabinet. In those trying days just before the completion of the Constitution of 1917, when internal dissension was most dramatically shown by Pancho Villa's activities and when the threat of active intervention by the United States was very real in Mexico— Pershing was even then leading the Punitive Expedition—Cabrera attempted to explain the Mexican Revolution in terms which could be comprehended by the citizens of the United States. He and three other Mexicans appeared before a joint meeting of the American Academy of Political and Social Science and the Pennsylvania Arbitration and Peace Society, held in Philadelphia on November 10, 1916. He was at that time the Minister of Finance in Carranza's government.

THE [Mexican] people saw that it was impossible to transform anything by peaceful methods. They had then to resort to force in order to destroy a régime which was contrary to their liberty, development and welfare. The last six years of internal upheaval, though chaotic in appearance, mean for Mexico the sociological transformation of her people. . . .

It has been said that the Mexican Revolution is not properly a revolution, but mere anarchy, that countries at peace consider dangerous and intolerable. Nevertheless, if we can demonstrate with facts that the Mexican Revolution has followed exactly the natural course of any other revolution, and if it can be demonstrated that even at the present time the revolutionary government of Mexico is pursuing a well defined program of reconstruction, one must necessarily reach the conclusion that the Mexican people are not acting madly, nor blindly destroying her wealth and her men, but

performing a task of transformation beneficial and indispensable, from which results may be expected that will be commensurate with the sacrifices that are now being made. . . .

When a system of work is right, but we fail to obtain results from our efforts for lack of efficiency, the task of the reformer consists in improving that system. But when a system is radically wrong, we must abandon that system and find a better one. The gradual and slow reform of a system to make it suit the requirements of a man, of a business enterprise, of an institution or of a country, is called *evolution*. The abandonment of a system to be replaced by another, is called a *revolution*. The use of force is not essential to a revolution; but the revolution in the personal conduct of men, in business or in communities, implies always a considerable effort and a great amount of sacrifice.

Historically, we can assert that with very

From Luis Cabrera, *The Annals* (January 1917), pp. 11–17. Reprinted by permission of the publisher, The American Academy of Political and Social Science.

1

few exceptions, the greatest conquests of human liberty and human welfare have not been made without large sacrifices of men and property. Sociologically, the revolution is the rebellion of a people against a social system that has been found wrong. But as every social system is embodied in certain laws and in a certain political organization, revolution appears always as a violation of existing laws and as an insurrection against the Government. Hence all revolutions appear as anarchical attempts to destroy society and this is also why most insurrections are called revolutions.

A revolution means the use of force to destroy an unsatisfactory system and the employment of force and intelligence to build the new system. A revolution has consequently two stages clearly defined; the destructive, which is nearly always a period of war and rebellion against the so-called established Government, and the stage of disavowal of most of the existing laws, which means the use of force against the social, economic and legal system.

When the old régime has been destroyed, the mere reëstablishment of legal order without any change, would be tantamount to the simple reconstruction of the same structure already destroyed. This is what sometimes makes revolutions fail. To avoid this, any revolution has a second stage that is always known as the period of revolutionary government. During this second period, force is also employed in the form of a dictatorial government, to establish the required reforms, that is to say, to lay the foundations of the new social, economic and political structure. After every revolution, a period of dictatorial interregnum has always followed, because revolutionary dictatorship means the use of force for reconstruction.

When the foundations of reconstruction have been laid down, then it is possible to return to a legal régime no longer based upon the old legislation nor upon the obsolete system, but upon new principles that become the new legal system, that is to say, the new régime. The French Revolution has been the most complete example of a revolution, with its frankly destructive period, its anarchic state, its revolutionary government and its new régime upon which France afterwards developed and we also can say upon which the rest of Europe has subsequently developed.

The Mexican Revolution was nothing more than the insurrection of the Mexican people against a very repressive and wealthy régime represented by the government of General Diaz, and against a social, political and economic system supporting such government. This revolution had as its prodrome the political insurrection of Madero. But Madero saw no more than the political side of the Mexican situation. He professed that a change of Government was sufficient to bring about a change in the general conditions of the country. Madero compromised with the Diaz régime, acquiesced in taking charge of his Government, and ruled the country with the same laws, the same procedure and even with the same men with whom General Diaz had ruled. The logical consequence was that Madero had to fail because he had not destroyed the old nor attempted to build a new régime. The assassination of Madero and the dictatorship of Huerta were mere attempts at reaction made by the old régime with its same men, its same money and its same procedure, and an attempt to reëstablish exactly the same old conditions that existed during General Diaz' rule.

The Constitutionalist Revolution set forth from the very beginning its line of conduct. The Plan of Guadalupe issued by Mr. Carranza in March, 1913, immediately after the assassination of Madero, is the straightest revolutionary proclamation that could be imagined to destroy an old régime. This plan meant the absolute disavowal of the executive, legislative and judicial powers that had existed up to that time, and authorized the use of force for the destruction of Huerta's government, which was being supported by General Diaz' army, by the power of the landowner and by the moral influence of the Catholic clergy.

A period of bloody war followed, and when Huerta was finally defeated and the chief of the constitutionalist revolution reached the City of Mexico, it was believed that the destructive period of the Mexican Revolution was at an end. But a period of an extremely chaotic and anarchic character necessarily followed. At the end of 1914 the Mexican situation was most puzzling and bewildering, and still it was at that very moment and in the middle of such an extreme confusion, that Don Venustiano Carranza, as the chief of the Constitutionalist Revolution, set forth the general outlines upon which the reconstruction of Mexico was to be carried out.

These outlines are embodied in the decree of December 12, 1914, which I will quote here as the best interpretation of the basic lines upon which the new régime and the new social system were to be found. The decree in substance indicates that whereas the use of force had been required to overthrow the Huerta Government in view of the chaotic conditions of the country, it was necessary to use the same force to continue the struggle until peace should be attained, and to reconstruct the new régime.

The main provisions of said decree read as follows:

ARTICLE 1. The Plan of Guadalupe of the 26th of March 1913 shall remain in force until the complete triumph of the Revolution. Consequently Citizen Venustiano Carranza will continue as First Chief of the Constitutionalist Revolution and in Charge of the Executive Power of the Nation, until such time as the enemy is vanquished and peace is restored.

ART. 2. The First Chief of the Revolution, in Charge of the Executive Power, will issue and put in force during the struggle all such laws, regulations and measures that may satisfy the economic, social and political requirements of the country, carrying out such reforms as public opinion may require to establish a régime to guarantee the equality among all Mexicans, to wit: Agrarian laws that may facilitate the creation of small property, parcelling the large estates and restoring to the villages the commons of which they were un-

justly dispossessed; fiscal laws tending to reach an equitable system of taxation upon real estate; legislation to better the condition of rural laborers, working men, miners and in general of all the proletariat; establishment of municipal liberty as a constitutional institution; basis for a new system of organization of the army; reform of the electoral system to obtain actual suffrage; organization of an independent judicial power both in the Federation and the States; revision of laws relating to marriage and civil status of persons; regulations that will guarantee the strict enforcement of the Reform laws; revision of the civil, criminal and commercial codes; reformation of judicial proceedings for the purpose of obtaining a rapid and efficient administration of justice; revision of laws relative to the exploitation of mines, oil, waters, forests and other natural resources of the country, in order to destroy monopolies created by the old régime and to avoid the formation of new monopolies in the future; political reforms that may guarantee the real enforcement of the Constitution of the Republic, and in general of such other laws as may be considered necessary to ensure to the inhabitants of the country the real and full enjoyment of their rights and equality before the law.

ART. 4. At the triumph of the Revolution, when the Supreme Power be reinstated in the City of Mexico and after municipal elections take place in most of the States of the Republic, the First Chief of the Revolution, in Charge of the Executive Power, will call elections for the Federal Congress fixing the proclamation, the dates and conditions in which said elections must take place.

ART. 5. When the national Congress assembles, the First Chief of the Revolution will report to it concerning his stewardship of the power vested upon him by this decree, and he will especially submit the reforms issued and put in force during the struggle, so that Congress may ratify, amend or supplement them, and raise to the rank of constitutional provisions such laws as may have to take that character; all before the establishment of constitutional order.

The reading of this decree is of the utmost importance to all who seem to be confused by events developing in Mexico since the overthrow of Huerta, and to those who see in Mexico only an incomprehensible condition of anarchy. It will be of still greater importance to know that this decree has been the rule under which the construction of Mexico is being made by the Revolutionary Government. . . .

If Carranza and the men around him are personally overpowered by the new anarchic period, and if they have to die or get out, that would not mean that my conclusions are wrong. It would only mean that a man is not always a span between two régimes. There have been cases in which a revolution has been completed during the life of a man, be he Cromwell or Washington. At other times a long list of heroes and martyrs is required to complete a transformation of the people, from Mirabeau to Napoleon.

In Mexico we have had three revolutions. Our revolution of independence in 1810 was not carried out by a single man. Hidalgo initiated it and died without seeing the end. Morelos continued it and also passed away before our country was free. Guerrero was the only one who saw the consummation of our independence. In 1857 it took only Juarez to see the beginning and the end of the reform revolution. The present revolution has already consumed Madero. If Carranza does not see the end of this movement, that will not change the development of the revolution. It will only mean that Carranza himself and the men around him are no more than a link in the chain of men who will sacrifice their lives for the liberty and the welfare of the Mexican people.

Bernard Shaw says that revolution is a national institution in England, because the English people, through democratic proceedings, can make a revolution every seven years, if they choose to do so. The Anglo Saxon referendum is no more than a right to peaceful revolution. The Mexican people do not enjoy that blessing, and have been obliged to engage in a bloody and costly revolution to attain their liberty and welfare. . . .

A revolution is not always a source of evil and tears, just as fire does not always produce devastation. Unexplored wildernesses of the Temperate Zone can be opened to agriculture by exploiting the forest wealth and at the same time preparing the soil for future cultivation. In tropical countries, however, the common way of opening fields to cultivation is to clear them with a great fire that consumes indeed much natural wealth, but which at the same time devours rapidly the jungle and by purifying and fertilizing the soil, saves a large amount of work.

The Revolution Was Fought to Equalize Capital and Labor

NICOLÁS CANO

To Nicolás Cano, a Guanajuato miner and labor leader, the aim of the Revolution was clear: justice for the working man. Cano sat mute through thirty days and thirty-nine sessions of the Constitutional Congress in late 1916, days of incessant wrangling and sessions of bitter in-fighting. He listened to the big guns of the Revolution while they expounded their reasons for supporting this doctrine or rejecting that; he heard flights of oratory with historical and literary allusions which he did not comprehend, and the constant repetition of such words as "liberty," "freedom," "justice," and "liberal." But he heard no satisfactory discussion of the elementary rights of the laboring man.

A simple man, he gave no polished peroration; a suspicious man, he wanted from the constitution nothing save the right for the worker to be treated equally under law with management. The following speech, his only one in the first half of the convention proceedings, was made on December 22, 1916. It is repetitious, filled with incomplete thoughts and dangling clauses, and very formal. Cano was uncomfortable on the podium, but he expressed a widely held point of view.

At issue in the fortieth session was Article 9, which concerned the right of assembly. The Constitution of 1857, Carranza's draft for a new constitution, and the proposals made by the convention's Drafting Committee all contained an almost identical first paragraph assuring the right of peaceful assembly for lawful purposes. But Carranza's second paragraph gave to public officials the authority to dissolve assemblies gathered for an "unlawful object" or in which there were "armed individuals," and the Drafting Committee's second paragraph opened the way for similar action in case of "violence or threats." Cano saw these provisions as threats to the right to strike, the workers' only weapon.

ONLY the worker can obtain an improvement in the worker's condition. I have studied the proposal which the First Chief [Carranza] has presented, and while the worker is scarcely benefitted, the militant groups in the country are given privileges and other groups are given privileges so that the political life of the nation may be in greater harmony, but regarding the worker, he was hardly remembered.

Article 9 is truly prejudicial for us the workers. The precept in the Constitution of 1857 is very broad, because it has no limitations; it says that persons may gather for lawful purposes, except when they are armed, and does not put restrictions. The second paragraph of Article 9 of Carranza's proposal, which the Drafting Committee with good judgment left out, undermines fundamental rights. The second paragraph of the Drafting Committee's proposal also undermines those rights, and the same reasons which may be considered for the first are true for the second, for from the moment any public official is given the opportunty to say whether a meeting is lawful or unlawful, we are very close to arbitrariness; I am going to discuss the question only from the point of view of the

worker, and for this purpose I am going to cite for you two cases to support my point.

I am going to cite them briefly so as not to waste time. I propose to this honorable assembly: that strikers not be declared alterers of public order or of peace. The reasons I have for asking this are the following: the strike which took place in Mexico City in the middle of this year, as you know, concluded with the shooting of some organized workers. I am not going into the question of why, when and how they were shot. Reasons could be given both for and against, but the fact is they were shot and against this act comes my protest as a worker. When the workers called the strike, the authorities immediately called out sufficient forces to prevent disorder, which might or might not have taken place; but it went no further, and concluded with the shooting of some of the workers. This situation, viewed from the point of view of the worker, is unjust.

Now I am going to cite a case on the other side. About three months ago the mining companies which operate in the state of Guanajuato stopped all work; we, gentlemen, seeing that misery would come to us, because Guanajuato is essentially a

From Nicolás Cano, *Diario de los debates del congreso Constituyente* (Mexico, 1922), Vol. I, pp. 607–610, 616. [Editor's translation.]

consuming city, it is only a producer of silver, it was impossible for fifteen or sixteen thousand workers to live, taking into consideration that the workers have the lowest wages, taking into consideration that the laborer in Guanajuato is among those having the least savings, and so we approached the authorities and through the state government we were able to get free passes so that the workers with their families could leave the city of Guanajuato. Fifteen or sixteen thousand people left; but on the other hand those of us who stayed were in frightful condition. Believe me, gentlemen, it was rare in those days when there were not one or two deaths daily from hunger. I have seen them taking little children of eight or ten years of age to the hospitals, with the bones held together only by the skin. The major portion of the deaths were brought on by the poor quality of the food. With this came need, and the typhoid has come and brought real atrocities. The city is dead and he who does not want to believe it need only go and see, and see if beholding it does not break your heart.

We have done all that is possible to get the mining companies to operate. You will realize that even with such a terrible experience we could not make use of the penal code, and you will also understand what we could legally do. We went to the companies, we talked to the management, we had conferences with the governor, we sent commissions to Mexico City, which were not received because of lack of time and because they could not defray all the expenses which they would have to meet and, finally, we did all we could. In the last meeting held in the Juárez Theater a few days before November 20 [when I left to come to this Convention], the situation was really desperate, and this was the last recourse we had. Some of us got together and we asked those few companions who remained there to come, and through the secretary of government we asked the [mine] managers to come. One or two came, and there we explained to them that

the situation was desperate and that they had an obligation to open the mines, since there was no reason for not working them. They gave only pretexts. When we said to them why were the mines not working, they answered that the [proportion of] zinc, hydrochloric acid and many other substances had increased, and we answered: "Gentlemen, we do not have all the facts necessary to be able to know whether you are right or not when you tell us that you cannot work the mines. We would have had to manage this business for some time in order to see whether it was worth working them or not." In the last interview we had with them, we told them the following: "You cannot work the mines, because you say the metals do not produce enough, and since we cannot make you work the mines, nor can we demonstrate the opposite of what you tell us, we will say this to you: you can give us the mines on shares, which would not mean any expenditure for you. You have dynamite, you have twenty-three thousand kilograms; you have twenty-two thousand feet of fuse and seven thousand detonators, and so on, and so you have all the materials necessary to work the mines for a long time. Furthermore, with the work on shares which we propose to you, the mine need furnish only the mine and the steel and the forges, and the miner will undertake to furnish the powder, candles, fuses and his work. Accordingly the company cannot allege that it does not have enough raw materials for this work." I said to them: "Gentlemen, if you also argue, as you surely will do, that the mines worked on shares will be greatly damaged, I will say to you: I propose that you name three engineers who will be those in charge of the work and that they say where, when and how these mines should be worked so that you will not run the danger that they will be destroyed." They could not allege that the mines were not in condition to be worked, since as soon as they received an order from New York they would put them to work. They have not prohibited them from being operated; when they saw that they had absolutely no answer, they said: "Gentlemen, we will consult New York, and as soon as they answer by cable, we will give you the answer." From the seventeenth of November until today many days have passed and we have had not a single word.

In one of the earlier strikes we said that it was impossible to live on three "unfalsifiable" paper pesos, or Veracruz bills.[1] We were told that they could not pay us more and that to prove it they were going to ask New York for the latest reports, which gave the reasons they could not pay dividends. We told them, "You cannot pay dividends not because the company is not in condition to pay them, but because you will use the money for other things; but, just the same, let us see the report." That was six months ago, gentlemen, and we have had no report.

Now then, as you know we are legally authorized to work those mines; article 11 [of the Constitution of 1857] clearly says: "The mines," not literally, but this is the sense of it, "the mines that bring a profit, and whose owners do not want to work them, will be declared of public utility." And gentlemen, in the city of Guanajuato, which lives solely and exclusively from the mines, are they of public utility or not? Yes, it is clearly so, since a city which lives exclusively from the mines and loses that industry, that city dies, as the city is dead at the moment. Now then, gentlemen, there has been no way to make them work. I do not ask, as some of my companions who have asked for privileges for the newspaperman, who have asked for juries for the newspapermen [for privileges]; I ask only that we be given justice.

If we cannot legally obligate the owner of an enterprise to operate his business for this, that, or the other reason; and if we set neither soldiers nor public authority against him, then I want the worker to have his right to strike respected, the more

so since, gentlemen, in spite of what they tell us, very few of the strikes in this country have been disorderly. The first time we went on strike in Guanajuato, we named a commission which went about asking for donations to help sustain the poorest of our companions. We gave each of them a peso every three days from the provisional government, and thus we sustained ourselves for nine days and nevertheless, there was not a single petty thief and you know that a people who give proof of such good judgment and honesty merits respect. We do not ask you to give us privileges, merely that we be treated the same as the capitalists, since we are the workers and do not want the privileges to be given only to them.

We sent a commission to Mexico. First of all we did not have the money and to all the sources to which we went to solicit funds, it was not possible for them to give us anything at all. Those of us who were dying of hunger and in misery, gentlemen, I and many of our companions, when we went out to work in the morning we had a breakfast of a piece of bread of a hundred-fifty grams and a cup of corn gruel. Look, gentlemen, about the fifteenth or sixteenth of November the naming of a commission was approved, but it did not go to Mexico because it could not. It was given a subsidy of seventy "unfalsifiable" paper pesos, when in Silao it was at the rate of a hundred to one. The subsidy of seventy pesos was given for three men. In Silao, in the most humble manner in the world, they had breakfast; they spent nineteen pesos for it. How would you have them continue? If we did not have even the money for a stamp for a letter, do you think we would have enough for a telegram? Furthermore, all kinds of approaches were made to the governor of the state; this was proposed to him: "Would you like, governor, to influence the central government so that these mines can be worked on shares, so that the income might be used to guarantee the value of the 'unfalsifiable' paper money, which now has no guarantee?" He did not pay any attention to us, either. I think this

[1] Issued in early 1916, these bills had depreciated to a value of about one centavo in mid-November; at the time the strike began, they were worth about six U.S. cents. [Editor's note.]

was a practical suggestion; furthermore, to work in this fashion no capital would be needed because they would have to do no more than open the mines, and then when the workers took out the metal they could then decide whether or not it would be wise to buy it. There is more, gentlemen; those who used to buy the ores [from the workers who picked over the abandoned wastes] have recently refused to do so. I submit this to your consideration as a mining engineer [said to another member of the assembly]: for more than fifteen days now no one has bought a single piece of ore. Now then, for those poor men who lived from this source, how would you have them live now? They have been earning, each one, no more than six and a half pesos every two weeks; do you think a man can live on three and a half pesos a week? Perhaps if he is alone; but if he has a family? Look, gentlemen, at the Burgos works; I have seen this: that the totality of the men, the common laborers, eat this: a handful of toasted corn. Nevertheless, gentlemen, not a single case of robbery has taken place, and you know that a people who are so good, deserve guarantees. But gentlemen, in spite of all this, I assure you that the day that those few inhabitants remaining in Guanajuato dying of hunger, in a moment of desperation they might have on seeing their children dying of hunger, go out and steal a bit of bread, they will fall under the sanction of the laws and they will be shot.

Well then, gentlemen, for that reason I ask for this, that for the same reason that machine guns are not used to make a mine owner work his mines, that the workers not be prevented from striking, for it is not just that a worker will be sent to jail because he commits a minor disorder or goes on strike. We in Guanajuato, the first time we went on strike we were three thousand of us and we did not make any trouble at all, because all of you know that those who cause the trouble during strikes are those paid by the companies, who pay the trouble-makers in order to give a pretext to the authorities to stop the strikes, and we are

not to blame at all. What I refer to is this, gentlemen of the Assembly: whether a strike demonstration should be considered a breach of the public peace, and, therefore, should be dissolved by the authorities; because there are cases in which the strikers, for example, go to prevent the others from working and it is said that this attacks the rights of third parties. The men always go to convince the others in a good will; four or five men are named to start the strike, always being just, and these men are then named to go to see the rest who want to enter to work, preventing them from working, and this is what the authorities use to dissolve it, alleging that they are the disturbers of the peace, and they dissolve it. I respectfully ask this Assembly to take this into consideration and to state that no strike may be broken up [by the government] and that the workers not be considered as disturbers of public peace.

Regarding the First Chief's proposal, it is also dangerous, for while the first clause says what is lawful, the other says what is unlawful, and to leave to a public official the designation of what is lawful and what is unlawful, that is very bad. I disagree with this, gentlemen; men do not change in five minutes and I ask you, gentlemen, to leave the article as it is in the Constitution of '57, since that is a full and complete article, and it has no restrictions, it is not ambiguous, but it is clear and conclusive and leaves the subject perfectly well-defined and gives no room for bad interpretations. When you find an unscrupulous governor, he perverts a [constitutional] article even if it is good, and this you gentlemen know.

I knew what would happen here, but I did not want to see it happen. It is too bad that in a body such as this where, it is thought, the most select and the most illustrious men in the nation come, they come here with trivial reasons and subjects.

We, from whom precious time is being taken, we who have no other desire than to work, if we come here, we come looking for good and sensible legislation which will give us guarantee. We who come here, not with illusions, we who have no illusions because we know that the Government, the Clergy and the capitalists are the natural enemies of the workers, and that it is impossible to find one without the other, undoubtedly should seek the greatest harmony in the present historic moment; but this does not mean that they are going to be our friends — never! You know that it is a great truth that so long as you try to bring about an understanding between dissimilar things, we cannot seek for legislation which will make us great and strong. Thus I am very sorry that so much time is being lost here in defaming and in insulting one another. We, the underdogs, who are far from all this kind of rottenness and who, when we feel something, when we want to say something we find that person and we say to him: you are a this and a that and another thing. And so it is gentlemen, that I leave this platform with the hope that you take into consideration the reforms which I propose, because it is just. I do not ask for anything out of the ordinary; I ask only that you equalize us with the capitalists, that if you do not force a capitalist to operate [his business], then that you do not attack the worker when he goes on strike, either.

The Revolution Was Fought for Democracy

ALVARO OBREGÓN

Alvaro Obregón, one of the great heroes of the military struggle against both Huerta and Villa, supported Carranza until 1917 when differences of political philosophy and action necessitated his resignation from the government. He then returned to Sonora, his native state, where he quietly raised chick-peas and just as quietly observed the national political scene, waiting more or less patiently for the election of 1920 at which time he fully expected to be chosen president without opposition. But Carranza had plans which excluded Obregón from the presidential chair, forcing the Sonoran into an opposition candidacy. In a manifesto announcing his determination to enter the political lists, Obregón viewed the Revolution as basically political; implicit in his position is an assumption that the Mexican people, given an opportunity to express themselves through the polls, would support legislation and administrative action putting into effect the social and economic provisions of the Constitution of 1917. The manifesto itself, however, makes no mention of land reform, labor laws, anticlericalism, education, or the other aspects of the Revolution as it has developed. This statement, the most important national pronouncement which Obregón had made to date, seemed to say that the essential aim of the Revolution was to give the majority of the Mexicans a voice in government.

EVEN in this retreat where I had hoped to make my life one of dedication to work and of domestic tranquility, there has been felt in these past few months something akin to the surge of the sea reaching the beaches when the depths are disturbed; and this disturbance, which at first appeared to be slight and of no importance, has grown so

From Alvaro Obregón, *La Caída de Carranza: de la dictadura a la libertad*, ed. José Vasconcelos (Mexico, 1920), pp. 3–26. [Editor's translation.]

in the past few weeks that it has caused serious preoccupation on my part.

In the beginning there were a few letters, principally from my friends, hinting to me that I should come out of my refuge and prepare to enter the political contest which is nearing; and as I write this, innumerable such hints arrive from friends, from unknown persons, from labor groups, from representatives of political groups, etc., etc., and, finally, some political parties in different parts of the country have launched my candidacy for the Presidency of the Republic for the next constitutional term.

The communications I receive on the matter differ greatly in form; some come in a tone of supplication, others in an imperative tone, some pointing out to me my historic responsibilities if I proclaim my abstention from the political contest, etc.; and those in whose name they say they come are even more varied: they speak to me in the name of the Motherland, of Democracy, of the group of which they are the officers, in the name of the Revolution, etc.

I must, then, submit to my judgment the task of resolving which road duty points out to me, since it is impossible to remain indifferent to the situation which approaches; and, counselled by that judgment, I will seek the place where I belong so that I might take it without vacillation.

It has been scarcely two years since constitutional rule was returned to the Nation, restoring to us all the rights which had been snatched away by the usurpation, and I wanted to be one of the first to enjoy those rights inasmuch as they signify a legitimate triumph gained by the sacrifice of all our comrades killed in the struggle, and so I gladly renounced all the trappings of the soldier to which my duty subjected me for a number of years.

It has been scarcely two years that I have lived in legitimate well-being, and now I must begin an interruption filled with anxieties, responsibilities and dangers, in order not to break the bonds which link me with duty.

In order to determine the place where I belong, I must make a careful examination of the causes which give rise to the uneasiness which is being felt and the anxieties awakened by the approaching electoral campaign in which the people must designate the successor to the present President of the Republic.

How many political parties are there now in the country, and what are their leanings?

There is only one active party, and its leanings are progressive, but it is divided into an infinity of groups which differ among themselves only in details which might be better considered as variants reflecting the character of their organizers.

How many political parties have there been in the country?

Only two: the Conservative Party and the Liberal Party, with diametrically opposed tendencies.

How are these two parties distinguished?

Ever since our country began its first liberating movement, the Mexican family has been divided into two political parties, one formed by the oppressors and the other by the oppressed, the first taking the name of Conservative and the second that of Liberal. The first was made up of: the opulent, the upper clergy, the privileged foreigners; the second: all the working classes — day-laborers, workers, professionals, small agriculturalists, ranchers and shop-owners — constituting the great majority of the Mexican family, whose power has been demonstrated clearly in the armed conflicts, from which they have invariably emerged victorious in spite of the disadvantageous position in which they have always found themselves on starting the struggle.

What other elements have aided the Conservative Party?

In every movement coming after that of Independence, the Conservative Party has seen itself reinforced by the leaders of the Liberal Party who, blinded by ambition or in defense of illicit fortunes, have prostituted their fame, and these men have generally been used by the Conservative Party as vehicles through which it comes to power. This type of Neo-Conservative has always been the most serious block to the realization of liberal principles.

Why does the Liberal Party lose in the political struggles which follow armed victory, even though this party represents the great majority?

Because when the political struggle is initiated, it is always done within the party itself and the party disintegrates, producing divisions which may be seen in both general and local aspects: the first may be considered as those produced throughout the country, their number always determined by the number of military leaders at the conclusion of the armed conflict who are considered as presidential material; with regard to the second, they are produced in an identical way in each state.

[The party loses the political contest through] the loss of repute which some of the leaders, especially the outstanding ones, bring to their party when they depart from the road which principle points out, in order to follow a path which leads to opulence and power, taking advantage of the fame gained through collective force to obtain fortunes and to commit injurious acts, acts which are condemned by Public Opinion for the good of the Motherland.

What is the situation of the Liberal Party at the moment?

Disastrous.

The Liberal Party is practically disintegrated, because on this occasion all the phenomena which I have pointed out as factors in earlier failures have been repeated: the divisions have been produced in all their aspects, in many States of the Republic these divisions degenerating into armed conflict. . . .

What would be the situation of the Liberal Party if the Conservative Party, aided by the group of military leaders mentioned in

the above paragraph, brings one of these leaders to supreme power over the nation?

Impossible.

Because the Liberal Party, disintegrated as it is, would see itself abandoned by a great number of those who now call themselves its leaders and who are even now growing away from it, for they would of necessity have to become a part of the Establishment in order to safeguard their interests; and this would leave the bitterest of choices to those independent groups and military leaders who have not violated their honor and who have resisted the temptations of easy money: either join the ranks of the skeptics and retire to their homes, where a mysterious death might come to them,[1] or to take up arms again and once more light the flames of a civil war which would undoubtedly be the bloodiest ever, because it would take on an avenging aspect, thus putting thousands of lives, immense property and perhaps even the national being itself in danger.

What would be the future judgment concerning the constitutionalist revolution and its first chief if the Conservative Party were able, through the complicity of the chieftains I have mentioned, to control the nation and to destroy the revolutionary work seen in nascent legislation?

Fatal.

It is generally accepted that the First Chief of the Constitutionalist Army was very lenient with the military leaders, particularly in questions of personal acquisitions, because he believed that the only objective during the fighting was the overthrow, by means of armed force, of the usurper Victoriano Huerta, first, and to subdue the traitor Francisco Villa later, leaving the moralizing and corrective acts to be put into effect after the establishment of a Constitutional Government and when he could count on greater authority.

Afterward, it has been believed that the

---

[1] There had been a number of assassinations — some of Obregón's friends and some of his enemies — since 1916. [Editor's note.]

acts of corrections have been postponed owing to the difficult conditions with which the government has had to contend, leaving them to be more easily carried out by a successor who would have no political commitments to detain him.

But if in the end these men not only remain unpunished, but also control the government and are covering the vanguard of the Conservative Party which combatted the Revolution, then the fruits of those good seeds which the Revolution sowed and which have been irrigated by torrents of blood from unknown men will be destroyed just when they are ready for harvesting; and then a justified protest of indignation will gush forth from all parts of the Republic against the leaders of an armed movement which bloodied and desolated the country for so many years, which dislocated the normal order of things, to produce as its only and bitter fruit a group of ambitious men who took for their own the nation's power and wealth.

What are the causes of the uncertainty and anxiety which are presently sweeping the country?

There is a well-founded fear that the material interests accumulated by unscrupulous leaders during the Revolution signify an unsurmountable barrier to the implantation of those advanced principles proclaimed during the armed conflict, and most especially that which served as a fundamental base, which is the *effectiveness of the suffrage*.

There is, moreover, a legitimate desire on the part of the great majority to see themselves freed from any official tutelage at the time of voting, a tutelage which in our country has meant, as our bitter historical experience demonstrates, a guillotine for all public freedoms.

After having made the above observations, judgment becomes clear, pointing to the following conclusions:

I. There is a great anxiety all over the country, because it is deeply feared that the right to vote, the principle that has served as the cardinal point of the armed movement, will be held up by the barrier presented by the material interests accumulated by many of the principal *caudillos* and leaders during the Revolutionary period.

II. There is a well-founded fear that a political failure on the part of the Liberal Party will give the Conservative Party the opportunity to destroy the incipient reforms, the majority of which have not yet been put into practice, but are the anxiously awaited fruit of the Revolutionary movement. . . .

III. There is a great anxiety, too, because it is felt that peace will be endangered if the people see themselves defrauded of their supreme desires, which have been the only emollient to attenuate their sufferings and miseries during the struggle.

IV. The Liberal Party, in whose custody the national dignity has always been held inasmuch as it has been the only one which has nobly defended that dignity with its blood when it has been threatened by foreign armies drawn [to the country] through the deceit of the Conservative Party, is in danger because a few of its so-called leaders have perverted its principles and deserted its ranks.

V. The material interests created during the Revolution are the only obstacle to the implantation of the advanced principles which the Liberal Party proclaimed and defended with so much sacrifice during the recent struggle.

VI. Our rights as citizens are in danger.

VII. The historic figure of the First Chief of the Constitutionalist Army is in danger if his work . . . remains barren and comes solely to offer, as its bitter fruit, the doleful result of all our earlier revolutions; *not permitting the country to liberate itself from its liberators.*

Methods of averting the danger and of putting the Liberal Party in condition to obtain a definitive political victory.

I. By giving the Conservative Party an open opportunity to take part in the contest, within the ample breadth of our laws, without disguising itself behind the mask of the Revolution by presenting its program of retrocession and of oppression instead of a program produced by some Neo-Conservative.

II. By giving the means to every member of the Liberal Party of acting on his own initiative without subjecting himself to conditions stipulated by its directors. . . .

III. By initiating a new organization so that all the citizens of the Republic may cast their votes without the necessity of becoming a part of any of the groups which presently operate on the political scene, many of which are organized around official elements whose independence must be only relative.

Conscious of the dangers which I have pointed out and that threaten with death our rights as citizens, the dearest of principles for all of us who know how to esteem the honorable title of citizen, I . . . offer to my fellow citizens all my energies and my goodwill if they believe that at this time these endowments can mean a factor of union for all those citizens who, without moral or political laxity, want to combine their strength in defense of our national interests. . . .

Why have I not left the leadership of the contest with one of the militant groups which have offered me their support?

I. Because I am certain that the groups to which I refer should not be considered as political parties but as splinters of the Liberal Party, and to leave the leadership in the hands of these groups would be to provoke divisions within the party itself.

II. Because I am certain that the electoral triumph of any one of these groups would not give its candidate the moral strength necessary to confront the problems and to resolve them, or to avert the dangers which I have pointed out; only a frank manifestation of the national will can give this strength.

III. Because I am convinced that the most truthful interpretation. . . [of the

Revolution] lies in the promise of reconquering by armed force the rights violated by the usurpation, in order to return those rights to each and every citizen who could, soon and in the broadest sense, enter into the exercise of those rights; and this reconquest which, as I have said, should be considered fundamental, would be weakened if strength were given to the tendencies of any of the militant political groups which pretend to have the right to conduct politics only among those who took part in the armed conflict.

My firmest intentions on entering the coming electoral struggle as a candidate are:

I. To offer my services to the nation, as I am accustomed to do every time I see her institutions in danger.

II. To be relieved, in the case of an adverse decision, of the responsibilities which would weigh on me if in these moments I were to remain, through cowardice or selfishness, with an indifference which would be criminal.

I present myself, then, on the political stage to say to the nation: I am a candidate for the presidency of the Republic in the forthcoming election. I am under no commitments, of any nature, either within or outside the country.

I am not going to take the time to formulate a program full of mirages which would serve nought. I am convinced that the country does not want programs, which in the end are empty words. The people want action, and they want to find a successor to the present head of government who will inspire confidence, and my own antecedents are the only things which should serve as a basis for those who think it necessary to support me and for those who believe it best to fight me; and these antecedents are the best guarantee that my governing principle will be the most absolute respect for law under whose prerogative every inhabitant of the Republic, regardless of his political or religious creed, will have the same rights.

Nevertheless, I will now lay down some

general considerations regarding the problems which, in my view, constitute the core
from which all others derive.

The capital problems, as we may call
them, are two: the first of a moral and the
second of a political nature. I give greater
import to the moral, having a conviction
that without a base of morality no other
problem can be resolved.

The moral problem can be resolved only
if the successor to the present Chief Magis-
trate is sufficiently able to undertake an
energetic campaign of purification, beginning with the members of the army who
have abandoned the paths of honor, and
continuing it throughout the other branches
of the administration, applying it to all
those public functionaries who have
thought that the Revolution had as its only
end the enrichment of those who took part
in it. This task is indispensable after a
revolutionary movement in which, many
times, the necessities of the moment require
the utilization of men little experienced in
public affairs, and considerations for services rendered during a campaign demand
certain indulgences for military leaders and
others who give service.

In order for this task of purification to be
feasible . . . it is necessary that the successor
to the present President come to office without commitments of any kind, so that he
might have a broader field from which to
select those necessary for good services,
without being obligated to look for them
within a limited group.

*The problem of a political nature consists
of effective suffrage, and its favorable reso-
lution will automatically leave resolved
many others of capital importance.*

When the national and the state chief
executives and legislative representatives
can be elected by popular vote with absolute freedom, these men will then owe their
positions to the support of the people who
elected them and, consequently, will try to
live in accord with public opinion, sustaining and defending each and every question
which favors their constituents, whether it
be called the agrarian problem, a labor law,
or any other. But while a majority of these
executives or representatives owe their posts
to the support which their friendship with
high authorities gives them, they will take
care only to cultivate those friendships at
whatever cost . . . without considering the
necessities of their respective states or
districts. . . .

All of us, then, should act. We must not
contribute to a national disaster with our
criminal indifference. All of us should act,
I repeat, according to our political creeds.
I do not demand that everyone applaud and
adhere to this manifesto; I have too broad
a liberal spirit to want all to think the
same. That which I hold dear is that no
one show himself indifferent, and that all
enter into action when they have read this
manifesto; those opposed, to fight it with
all their energies and resources; those sym-
pathizing, to defend it and to sustain it
with all their resources and energies as well.

We must not lose sight of the fact that
only a decisive political action will resolve
the present national problem; without it,
the problem will remain and the consequences will be disastrous as our past, full
of bitter lessons, demonstrates for us.

It is time to act; the moment is solemn.
The future of our country will be determined in the approaching electoral contest.
Either our nascent democracy will be de-
finitively consolidated, closing the prolonged and shameful period of *coups d'etat*,
treasons and sharp practices, or the seeds
of the Revolution will be uprooted from
their natural beds and sowed in grounds
fertilized with abuse and immorality.

The Revolution Has Been Destructive

JORGE VERA ESTAÑOL

To Jorge Vera Estañol, a moderate *porfirista* who served in Huerta's cabinet, the Mexican Revolution from its beginning was something of a fraud; forty years after the drafting of the Constitution of 1917 his essential views had not changed. A firm believer in evolution, as opposed to revolution, Vera Estañol always held the conviction that the revolution in Mexico slowed down, rather than enhanced, an inevitable progress under the leadership of an enlightened upper class.

THE long road I have travelled for something over a half century of our national history, looking for truth unavailingly, without bias toward one ideology or another, without ingratiating myself with any political group or with the men who have formed them or do form them now, has taught me many worthwhile things which I am going to put into brief form.

One of these, the most fundamental, is that revolutions destroy, they do not create.

In countries of homogeneous civilizations, revolutions spring forth only when established institutions or the tendencies of the established government, or both, come into conflict with the status of the prevailing national consciousness, and in their immutability serve as a barrier to the progress of the people, sometimes because they encourage class hatred, sometimes because of anarchist attitudes toward cooperative activities, or sometimes because of unjust discriminations or persecutions.

The eminently destructive nature of revolution is, then, useful; when the obstacles are removed and the abnormal period of turbulence has passed, *the people can put into action their constructive potentialities*.

In hybrid societies, where the disparity of civilizations resists a synthesis toward a prevailing national consciousness, revolutions have their beginnings as mere symptoms of this cultural antagonism and, naturally, they either bring no permanent solution or they appear in chronic succession.

This is what happens in Spanish American nations, where two groups, one civilized and the other semicivilized, live together without fusing completely. For these nations of a heterogeneous ethno-socio-cultural complexion the only remedy is the elevation of the retarded masses by the means of education. . . .

Let us pass on to an examination of the fundamental promises of the revolution of 1910, complemented by those which the Constitution of 1917 contains.

UNLIMITED EFFECTIVE SUFFRAGE.
NO RE-ELECTION

Our people, unfortunately, have not been and are not prepared for effective suffrage, if by this we mean active, unlimited voting as a prerogative of a citizen.

About 28 percent of the inhabitants are members of the indigenous races; 5,227,396 according to the 1940 census.

There is no communion of aspirations, or customs, or necessities, or ideals, or of civilization between them and the rest of the population.

Forty-three percent of the Mexicans are fairly capable of feeling their nationality

From Jorge Vera Estañol, *La Revolución Mexicana; Orígenes y Resultados* (Mexico, 1957), pp. 763, 765, 767–772, 777–779. Reprinted by permission of Guadalupe M. de Vera Estañol. [Editor's translation.]

when holidays to commemorate heroes are celebrated, but they are incapable of understanding the economic-political-social necessities of the nation, and even less can they conceive of a way to satisfy them.

A minority — let us say, optimistically, thirty percent of the Mexican people — is capable of feeling and understanding the demands of a nation for its progress and for the realization of its historical destiny.

If to this portion of the public we were to limit exclusively the exercise of the franchise, then it would be possible, then suffrage would come to be effective and would allow the ignorant masses to become democratic, slowly extending the circle of voters through the civilizing action of education.

In all truth we must say, then, that the deviant revolutionary governments — we are not speaking of the revolution, since it ended with the adoption of the Constitution of 1917 — the deviant revolutionary governments, we repeat, have not fulfilled the solemn promise of *effective suffrage*, which served as an idea for involving the country in a fratricidal war after 1910.

And we are not the only ones who have made this accusation.

Emilio Madero — a revolutionist from 1910 — states his opinion thus on the failure: "I say that nobody in Mexico knows how the President is elected. In a true democracy it is done as it is here: the leaders of the parties meet and nominate their candidates, as we do here. But there they are extremely careful in doing so, because their nomination has to be approved by the public by means of the vote. But here, *No*. Here, once the official candidate is named there is no human power to oppose him. *There is no vote.*"

Revolutionist Marciano González, in a dinner given in honor of Rubén Morales, candidate for governor of Oaxaca, said: "A fraudulent failure has been made of the great ideals of the revolution, because democracy in Mexico is a lie, liberty a chimera, rights a sarcasm and effective suffrage a joke."

We do not tire of repeating it; Mexico

is not a democratic country: she aspires to be so, and this aspiration is extremely noble; but in order to achieve it, it is indispensable that we recognize, leaving aside considerations of a political order, that the suffrage be limited to the social classes capable of understanding — even though not very profoundly — the interests, aspirations and necessities of a nation and with a desire to extend the circle of these classes gradually, by means of education, until it includes the most distant corners and the highest mountains in the national territory.

The postulate of "no reelection" was only a battle cry against the continuation of Porfirio Díaz and Ramón Corral in power. This cry was not rooted deeply in our traditions, and was certainly not a part of the popular consciousness; nor did it have any meaning, if in truth effective suffrage were to be practiced.

For this reason Carranza, at the definitive triumph of the revolution, had himself reelected and changed only the name of his position.[1]

Ten years later it sufficed for Obregón, the most powerful leader of the revolution, to desire it and the Federal Congress — for the most part obsequious — along with the state legislatures approved, no less, an amendment to the brand new constitution again to permit reelection.

The people were not consulted nor were they disturbed by such revolutionary blasphemy, and it was necessary for an assassination[2] — completely foreign to the defense of the antireelectionist cause — to bring that chieftain's life to an end in order to allow the so often referred to second part[3] of the revolutionary motto to figure again in the Constitution.

Those who governed us then sought a

[1] Until March 1917, Carranza called himself the First Chief of the Revolution; he then became the President. [Editor's note.]

[2] Obregón served as president, 1920–24; he was followed by Calles, 1924–1928, and was then reelected, but he was assassinated before taking office. [Editor's note.]

[3] The motto is "Effective Suffrage, No Reelection." [Editor's note.]

means of perpetuating themselves in power without having recourse to reelection.

Carranza hoped to keep himself in power by initiating political heirdom, today known by the name of "continuity by deviousness"; but he lacked sufficient military power and paid with his life for his daring impudence.

The dynasty of Sonora then appeared with de la Huerta, continued with Obregón and, passing on to Calles, arrived at the "Exalted Leader" period.[4]

Calles tried to prolong it with Cárdenas; but the latter preferred, as did the Carolingians, to found his own dynasty; he ran the Merovingians out of the palace and under his political heirdom we have been living with Avila Camacho, Alemán and the present President.

How long will this Cárdenas "continuity by deviousness" last?

It is not now possible to predict; but it will not be the public, or any other democratic factor, which will bring it to an end; it will be done by a *caudillo,* or a high-flying politician, or a demagogue, sufficiently strong to dislodge the Carolingians and found the new dynasty of the Capetians.

Thus, of the two basic postulates in the political realm, the revolution *has not fulfilled and will not fulfill effective suffrage,* and for individual reelection it has substituted *continuity by deviousness,* which is nothing else than "dynastic reelection."

AGRARIANISM

The Agrarian problem is resolved by the Constitution! There is no more servitude on the soil, the farm laborer is the owner of the land, to him belongs all that Ceres, bountiful Ceres, can give to him; with one fell swoop the latifundia disappear and free citizens spring from the fields! All steadfast revolutionists and sham pseudo-revolutionaries proclaim it.

But the magic yardstick of Querétaro[5]

did not give the peasant money, nor implements, nor seeds, nor did it endow him with the necessary provisions; it did not create dams, canals, granaries; it did not build roads; it did not open up farm credit; it did not develop a coordination of the producers to assure a good market.

The farm laborer, standing on his land, felt isolated, unprotected, miserable, with a year ahead of him and not one ounce of corn with which to feed himself, and so he returned to serfdom or gave up country and everything else and began the fatiguing trek to the United States.

As we have said and repeat here: the State, the revolutionary tradition and the enticements of "continuity by deviousness" have sacrificed the country's national interest and its agricultural progress; the proof of this is that the production of land in Mexico does not now, given the growth in population and according to indisputable statistics, compare favorably with the production of fifty years ago.

We should, then, also recognize that the deviant revolutionary governments have not fulfilled the promise to improve the conditions of the peasant; they have not freed him from misery, nor have they emancipated him from the overseers; on the contrary they have created harder and crueler overseers — the *ejidal* managers — and yet more unjust and greedy masters — the agents of the Ejidal Bank.

And the pernicious influence of agrarian reform has not stopped here, since to date it has served only to apply the brakes to agricultural production, and in this manner has slowed the rise in the standard of living of our people.

It is necessary, it is imperative, that a government official of high political-social rank, a man of power, disavow the *ejidos* and bring them to an end forever.

LABORISM

Industrialization, around the turn of the century, received from the Díaz regime a major impulse.

With that development a strong feeling

[4] Calles, by Congressional action, was given the title of Maximum Chief of the Revolution. [Editor's note.]

[5] The Constitution of 1917. [Editor's note.]

of class was born and began to develop among the workers; as a consequence, shortly after the implacable destruction of the strikes at Cananea and Orizaba, the first labor organization appeared under the name of The House of the World Worker.

The movement, as a result of the country's ensuing industrial development and largely through the influence of the labor organizations of the northern neighbor which by a process of transudation crossed the border, continued to grow; consequently when the revolution triumphed there existed within the laboring class a collective consciousness and a determination of sustaining it through appropriate labor legislation.

The revolution demolished — and this is a permanently gained benefit — the wall which prevented the working man, that great factor of production, from being recognized as a collaborator and not merely a subordinate to capital, and permitted him to become organized into labor unions to demand his rights.

The revolution, nevertheless, has not been able to produce in these organizations a sufficient morality to create the development within the worker of a full consciousness of his own responsibility in perfecting his social function; but it is to be hoped that the seat of public power will give proper attention to this need, with the same tact that has been used by the present administration to reduce to a minimum the conflict between capital and labor, and to create between them an ambient of harmony, instead of the class struggle which has before prevailed.

Nor has the revolution been capable of destroying that breed of leaders, little and big, who now constitute a new class of overseers as hard and self-centered as were the old masters. The elimination of the closed shop would go far toward eliminating this evil.

The revolution indirectly permitted, through the development of group spirit among the workers, the creation and dispersion of productive cooperatives, concerning which the present problem is primarily to make them genuine cooperatives and to emancipate them from their new owners; that is, from the above-mentioned breed of exploitative leaders.

The humanitarian evolution of the feelings of our upper classes, and not the destructive force of the revolution, has been responsible for a great step forward in behalf of the worker, through the establishment and the steady broadening of social security.

STATISM

Apart from the powerful influence of the international atmosphere, which after the first world war began to favor directed economies on a grand scale, the principal internal cause of Mexico's adopting this path, and widening it day after day and year after year, can be found in the omnisocialistic policy which marked the Cárdenas presidential period.

The nationalization of the National Railways and the properties of the great oil companies signified for the government an enormous expenditure of money all out of proportion to the national resources and production, particularly since the two nationalizations followed a period of business paralysis brought on by capital's lack of confidence.

These two governmental monetary strictures coincided with the beginning execution of the agrarian policy, which demanded heavy money investments to supply the new landowners at the very moment when production was being lowered through the lack of capable field hands and adequate means to exploit the land.

To meet these imperious demands for money the government was forced to resort to, and did resort to, an alarming emission of paper money far in excess of that warranted by the economic conditions of productivity in the country; from this came inflation.

Following the Cárdenas administration, and during the regime of President Avila Camacho, public expenditures grew even more, under the pretext that the country was engaged in the Second World War —and I say pretext because our active participation in that war was limited to the formation and maintenance of our famous Squadron 201.

We declared war, nevertheless, and this allowed Avila Camacho to solicit and obtain extraordinary powers, and to exercise them in lavish fashion when it came to public funds; for under this administration the *nouveau riche* sprang forth with millions and millions in profits obtained through contracts and traffic with the federal government, and the inflation continued.

It did not stop here; mismanagement continued without let-up during the Alemán regime; the number of *nouveau riche* grew, as did the millions which they engrossed, money which could have come, and did come, only from the public coffers. New and still newer emissions of paper money were made to cover the deficit which this policy incurred and, finally, the peso dropped to 8.50 per dollar.

Successive peso devaluations brought in their turn, as a consequence, a great increase in the costs of articles of prime necessity. We can then repeat that the revolution has not brought greater well-being to the majority of the Mexican people, even though it has improved the condition of certain labor groups in the big cities.

But during the past two years, one can note a firm intention to augment agricultural and industrial production in order to remedy the ills we have pointed out. . . . Furthermore, in the last months of 1956 and up to the present time in 1957, some unmistakable rectifications have been noted on the part of our public officials, in the sense of recognizing that *individual initiative* must share in the economic redemption of the country and to that end they are consulting private institutions regarding economic questions and are opening to them the doors which will allow them to enter with their valuable and vital cooperation.

It is necessary to recognize, too, the efforts being made by the present government to consolidate the nation's international obligations as a means of encouraging the immigration of foreign capital, not only in government-owned enterprises but in private ones; this is an evolutionary policy, a policy clearly antirevolutionist and in open opposition to the Boxerism and the antiforeignism of which the drafters of the Constitution of 1917 were so proud.

We hope that this policy of rectification against revolutionary biases continues for the good of the country; that totalitarianism is gradually replaced by private initiative in all branches of production, to which end the following should be undertaken.

To dissolve those organs which have invaded the field of individual activity; or rather to allow their capital to be absorbed by private enterprise.

To suppress completely any control over prices, by guarantee or by any other form, which artificially impedes the free play of supply and demand.

To encourage investment of foreign capital, not so much in government or official works but in private areas, guarding only against a displacement of already-invested domestic capital, making it rather a cooperative endeavor, for which purpose it will be necessary to tear down the bars which have been created. . . .

SOCIAL DEMORALIZATION

We are not going to discuss the quantitative or saturation aspects of criminality in our country. We will leave that task to the specialists, so that it may be done with the presentation of appropriate statistics.

That which we wish to speak about, even though briefly, is that qualitative aspect of antisocial acts which blacken our national life.

It is not difficult to discover that the basis of these acts is an alarming degradation of that inner feeling built up in the souls of men over hundreds of centuries, that feeling which we call conscience and which allows us to distinguish good from evil, which commands us to help our fellow man rather than to do him harm, which orders us to live in harmonious neighborliness with our fellow man under the sublime maxim: "Love thy neighbor as thyself."

To what should we attribute this moral disorder which is unfortunately generalized throughout our society, particularly among the lower classes in the big cities?

Certainly the principal cause among us has been the armed struggles — call them revolutions, revolts or barracks uprisings as you will — which were an endemic condition for more than a generation after 1910.

From the slaughter on the battlefields, the mass executions, the plundering in cities, villages, hamlets and even private houses, there could only come hate, cupidity and all manner of unhealthy passions; in short, antisocial feelings.

Such confusion of conscience has invaded our society thanks to the rapid movement of the lower social strata, without proper educational preparation, into the higher levels; thanks to the considerable number and the aggressive spirit of the upstarts who clambered into political and social positions unfitted for them, an inherent phenomenon of any armed revolution.

Bloody assaults for the purpose of robbery have multiplied; these were so exceptional at the beginning of the century that they could be counted on the fingers of one hand; now they can be ticked off in shocking numbers: the murder of a chauffeur for the proceeds of one day's work; the forceful entry into a habitation in order to despoil an elderly person, or a woman, of life as well as goods; the malicious assault on a passerby, sometimes in broad daylight, also for the purpose of robbery.

All these crimes betoken that in the conscience of the perpetrators the I, that vile egotism, is so powerful that the sacrifice of an unknown life means nothing so long as a material advantage is gained, *so long as it makes a living for the criminal*.

When society is so profoundly contaminated, how deeply must the poisons have penetrated into the subordinate strata of our bureaucracy and the administration of justice! The lies, the briberies, the subornations, the immoral maneuverings which the government employees and the inspectors commit daily, and the cynical complicity of the police with the underworld, have come to seem to be small sins compared to the bloody crimes with which our society is saturated.

II. THE CHURCH-STATE CONFLICT

The Church Has Exploited the People

ARTURO M. ELÍAS

In January 1926, the tacit truce which had long existed between the anticlerical government and the Catholic Church hierarchy in Mexico came to sudden end amid recriminations from both groups. Since feelings ran high in the United States, and inasmuch as many important public figures were virtually demanding armed intervention, the contending parties were anxious to gain the sympathy and support from major segments of the population in the United States. Arturo M. Elías, Mexican Consul General in New York and a relative of President Calles, was prompt in expressing his government's position to the American public. His basic argument was that the events in Mexico were the logical consequence of centuries of exploitation by the Catholic hierarchy, which had always been a force for retrogression and a supporter of special interests destructive to the population at large.

THE Constituent Congress called to form a new constitution for Mexico met, just after the revolt, in 1856, in which the clergy, and particularly the Bishop of Puebla, took a leading part, had been put down by the new liberal administration. The cause of this revolt was the measure abolishing clerical and military privileges which had been drawn by Juarez, who was then the Secretary of Justice and Ecclesiastical Affairs.

There was no attempt on the part of the clergy to keep under cover during this revolt, and the friars of the monastery of El Carmen joined openly with the soldiery. The re-establishment of the ecclesiastical and military privileges was proclaimed by the insurgents, as well as the upholding of the Catholic religion to the exclusion of all others. President Comonfort led the loyal remnant of the regular army and a force of citizen followers against the seat of revolt, the city of Puebla. After fourteen days of desperate fighting, the Government forces carried the town, and the mutineers surrendered.

President Comonfort, in spite of the great loss of life and damage to property, issued a decree very mildly punishing the clerical leaders. His gentle treatment of the hierarchy, however, did not result in any change of heart on their part, and when the congress to fashion a new Constitution met, the clergy rallied all the forces of reaction back of their attempt to prevent any change in the laws which might interfere with their special privileges.

The bitterness of their opposition is shown by an incident which took place in the congress on the 30th of July, 1856. The day before, Francisco Zarco had made a very exhaustive and eloquent address on religious liberty in which he had indicted the Catholic Hierarchy for its intolerance and had made a special plea for full religious liberty. When the next day's session opened, it was found that the reactionaries

From Arturo M. Elías, *The Mexican People and the Church* (New York, 1926), pp. 15–23.

had filled the galleries with their followers. Soon there began to pour down upon the heads of the delegates broadsides bearing the printed words:

¡"Viva el Romano Pontífice y el clero"!
¡"El pueblo no quiere la tolerancia"!
¡"Mueran los enemigos de la religión Católica"!

(Long live the Roman Pontiff and the clergy! The people do not want tolerance! Death to the enemies of the Catholic religion!)

The Constituent Congress largely represented the growing liberal sentiment of Mexico. It was not in any sense opposed to religion. It did, however, stand for the right of everyone to worship God according to the dictates of his or her conscience. Its members had in the vast majority of cases been brought up in the Catholic faith, but were opposed to the special privileges given to the Catholic Hierarchy.

Bitter experience had determined them to curb the power of the Church authorities, and thus open the way for a larger political, intellectual and spiritual freedom for the Mexican people. Their true sentiments can be found in the preamble to the new Constitution, which began with the sentence: "In the name of God, and by the authority of the Mexican people." They did not deny the claims of religion, but they did deny the right of the Catholic Hierarchy to be recognized as the only representatives of God in this world.

The first article of the Constitution shows the social vision which these men possessed. The first sentence in it read: "The Mexican people recognize that the rights of man are the basis and the object of social institutions." In a world that still condoned chattel slavery this assembly spoke out clearly against that iniquitous institution. Article 2 of the Constitution said: "In the republic all are born free. Slaves who set foot upon the national territory shall recover, by this act alone, their freedom, and enjoy the protection of the law."

The members of the Congress also showed to the world that they understood the vital importance of the development of knowledge if a free republic was to flourish and grow great, in the true sense of that word, for Article 3 began with the statement, "Instruction is free."

Two crushing blows were delivered at the power of the Church when the Constituent Congress passed Articles 13 and 27. The first dealt with the *fueros,* which can best be translated by "super-privileges." These super-privileges of the Church placed the priesthood absolutely outside of the power of the civil law. An ecclesiastical court existed, to which alone any member of the religious establishment was responsible. The military establishment also was free from civil control and responsible solely to the military courts. This power in the hands of the Church had been of vital importance to it in placing its yoke upon the shoulders of the Mexican people and keeping it there. The members of the Constituent Congress determined to tear out this iniquitous privilege root and branch, from the governmental system, and passed Article 13, which abolished the Ecclesiastical Courts. It read:

In the Mexican Republic no one shall be tried according to private laws or by special tribunals. No person or corporation shall have privileges nor enjoy emoluments which are not in compensation for a public service and established by law. Military jurisdiction shall be recognized only for the trial of criminal cases having direct connection with military discipline. The law shall clearly define the cases included in this exception.

The Committee of Justice in its report regarding the super-privileges enjoyed by the Ecclesiastics said that their abolition was imperative for two reasons: that their abolition was absolutely in accord with democratic principles, and that the special circumstances in which the Mexican people found themselves required their being swept away. "Without the abolition of these privileges," said the report, "democracy would be impossible, because the foundation of democracy is universal justice. Justice cannot be practiced if super-privileges for individuals or classes are recognized."

In another portion of the report the Committee called the attention of their fellow delegates to the fact that they all knew how difficult it was to obtain justice from the ecclesiastical or military courts, because of the favoritism shown to their own members by those who administered these courts. The revolt, led by the prelates of the Church, that had just been put down at Puebla was brought forward by the committee as an evidence of the danger of the special privileges given the Hierarchy. The committee asked:

Who can fail to lay a great share of the evils which we have suffered to the existence of these super-privileges and exemptions for the ecclesiastics — super-privileges that the enemies of progress are defending so strenuously? The committee is convinced that the existence of super-privileges is highly detrimental to the progress of the country.

It will perhaps be surprising to many to know that such super-privileges existed in a republic in the middle of the 19th Century. But, alas, for the prosperity and the happiness of the Mexican people, they did exist, and the attempt to abolish them bathed the soil of Mexico in the blood of its people, and those who were responsible for the death and misery brought upon the people were those who had used these super-privileges to eat out the very substance of the producing masses of Mexico.

That portion of Article 27 dealing with the Church said:

No religious corporations and institutions of whatever character, denomination, duration or object, nor civil corporations, when under the patronage, direction or administration of the former, or of ministers of any creed, shall have legal capacity to acquire title to, or administer, real property, other than the buildings immediately and directly destined to the services or purposes of the said corporations and institutions. Nor shall they have legal capacity to acquire or administer loans made on such real property.

The Congress tried to make this constitutional provision as sweeping as possible. Attempts had been made before to take back from the Church some of the immense wealth that had been absorbed through its enormous influence and the possession of super-privileges. This wealth had in turn been used to protect all these privileges. It must be wrenched from the greedy hands of the Hierarchy if any degree of democracy was to be realized by the Mexican people. It was all the fruit of the hard toil of the industrious masses, and the aim of the Congress was to return it to the people, organized as a nation. It was in no sense confiscation, but restitution.

The Church Hierarchy knew full well that its wealth gave it power over the lives of men, and that it could not hold its influence if it ceased to be the richest institution in the social system. It owned a great portion of best lands of Mexico, and where it did not directly own, it held mortgages on the land. It is small wonder that the Church's absorption of a great portion of the wealth of Mexico was denounced on the floor of the Congress as "a scandalous usurpation," when it is remembered that the Savior whom it pretended to represent on earth is described in the Gospels as one who "had no place to lay His head," and that the same Hierarchy hypocritically demanded from the priesthood the vow of "perpetual poverty."

It was Article 123 that brought down upon the framers of the Constitution a wrath which caused Pope Pius IX to fulminate against all the articles relating to the Church, declaring them "null and void"; a wrath which caused the Archbishop of Mexico to forbid citizens who were Catholics to take an oath of allegiance to the Constitution, and to order them, if they had already taken such an oath, to repudiate it in the confessional; a wrath which caused the Hierarchy to conspire and drive the President from his office, putting in his place Zuloaga, pledged to abolish all the provisions in the Constitution regarding the Church, as well as any other provisions of liberal tendencies.

The first paragraph of Article 123 said:

The Federal authorities shall have exclusive power to exercise, in matters of religious worship and outward ecclesiastic forms, such intervention as by law authorized.

Four amendments to this were added later, making the Church and the State independent of each other and forbidding Congress to enact any laws establishing or forbidding any religion; declaring marriage a civil contract; denying religious institutions the right to acquire real estate or capital secured by mortgage on same, except under the provisions of Article 27, and abolishing the religious oath, substituting in its place a simple promise to tell the truth and to comply with obligations entered into.

The Policy of the Government Is Anti-Religious

BISHOP PASCUAL DÍAZ

Pascual Díaz, one of the six bishops expelled from Mexico by the Calles government for seditious action which emanated from his statements on the duties of Mexican Catholics with respect to the government, was living in the United States when he was given the opportunity to express the Mexican Episcopate's viewpoint on the conflict. The account was hurriedly written in order to meet the publisher's deadline.

THIS struggle is not one of personalities. Above and beyond the bitter sayings and doings that such a situation always engenders, there is a serene plane of principles which are at variance. I can say for my part as Secretary of the Committee of the Mexican Episcopate that nothing but the compulsion of principle would have forced us to close the churches in Mexico and thus to deny to a whole people the consolations of their religion.

In point of fact there are two philosophies at grips today in Mexico. According to one of these, all rights enjoyed by citizens are derived from the State; they are a free gift by the community as such, they do not exist inherently in any individual or any group of individuals, and accordingly they can be revoked, or substantially curbed, at will by the State, which in practice means the Government of the State, though these two are not the same thing. Thus, beside the individual, the family, the school and the Church are all completely subject to the State in all things. This philosophy has found its flower in modern days at Moscow, for whereas its Nineteenth Century practitioners were stubbornly capitalist, the Bolsheviki logically added the right of property to the list of all the other rights residing in or deriving from the State, seeing no reason why it alone should be excluded.

The other philosophy professes that there are certain rights which reside inherently in the individual, the family, etc., and may not be destroyed by the State, which as represented in its Government exists solely

From Pascual Díaz, *North American Review* (April 1928), pp. 225, 401–408.

for the purpose of protecting them. This is the theory which I read clearly in the American Declaration of Independence, and which, I am told, is the constant idea behind the decisions of the American Supreme Court. It happens also to be the theory usually held by Catholics, and certainly held by those of us who, because of it, necessarily stood out against the Mexican Government whereas the other theory to a greater or less degree was espoused by those who followed Carranza in the so-called Constitutionalist movement of which he was the titular head, and of which Obregon and Calles are the successors. It is, therefore, the clash of these two philosophies which has caused the turmoil in Mexico these many years. Let us see how this clash has worked out in practice in the religious world.

In itself the Mexican Constitution of 1857, which was in force until 1917, was a sort of compromise between the theory of extreme State supremacy and the facts of Mexican civilization — if one sets aside the "Laws of Reform," added to the Constitution in 1873. The makers of that Constitution did not admit, for instance, that the Church had any inherent rights by virtue of its Divine foundation. Nevertheless, they conceded to it certain rights, *as if they were inherent*. By a legal fiction, they granted a juridical personality to the Church, so that it could own property, recover damages in law, defend its spiritual mission against aggression, conduct schools, be made the recipient of a legacy, dispose of property, and perform all the other acts which modern civilization concedes to any corporate body duly organized for a specific and legitimate purpose.

The Constitution of 1917 stripped the Church of every one of these rights, in general by denying to it any juridical personality, and in particular by a series of prescriptive and proscriptive regulations, which I shall relate in detail, and which were calculated in effect to reduce it to the condition of a mere appanage of the State.

This Constitution sets up absolute separation of Church and State, denying to Congress the right of establishing or prohibiting any religion whatever (Art. 130), and conceding to every citizen the right of professing, according to his conscience, any religion (Articles 24, 130). I will simply remark at this place that it is no part of the doctrine of the Catholic Church that where in a given country there does not exist religious unity, as in Mexico at present, there should be union of Church and State. This we expressly announced in our collective Pastoral of April 21, 1926, at which time we also said explicitly that for this reason not only were we not protesting against the above provisions of the Constitution, but that we accepted separation as the practical solution in the circumstances. The clash, therefore, did not arise over this point, as has sometimes been assumed.

This Constitution, however, went much farther than to decree mere separation of Church and State, and it is here the conflict took its rise. For it is one thing to separate Church and State; it is another to subject one of them to the other by law. Article 130 explicitly denies to all Churches any juridical personality, their universally recognized guarantee of independence from Government interference in purely spiritual matters and of constitutional protection against an invasion of their rights. In its place, the Constitution declares that the Federal authorities are empowered to exercise in matters both of worship and of external church discipline "the intervention which shall be designated by the laws." Later I shall show how the Enabling Act, a legislative decree framed and promulgated by the Executive, interpreted this intervention.

In consequence of this provision, the constitutional restrictions imposed on ministers of religion will not cause surprise. Clergymen are not to be recognized as ministers of religion, but as simple members of a profession, with important restrictions. They must be Mexicans by birth; their number in any locality may be limited by the State Legislatures; they are declared by the mere fact of their profession to have forfeited all their political or civil rights (Articles 82, 55, 59, 130: 3, 27). Their activity as ministers of religion is "fiscalized," that is, their control of church premises is a State function, shared by them with ten others, residing in the vicinity, or must be altogether transferred to other hands (Art. 130). A Mexican citizen, therefore, who becomes a clergyman, loses his legal existence as a citizen. Moreover, ministers of religion are restricted entirely to the "secular" clergy, for vows of religion and Religious Orders are altogether proscribed (Art. 5). It should also be remarked that these provisions do not apply exclusively to the Catholic Church, but to all religions alike.

In the provisions concerning marriage, public worship, education, the press, the church edifice, and church property in general, the same spirit predominates. Marriage is declared to belong to the civil power exclusively, and has only that validity which this power grants it (Art. 130). If it were merely declared that a civil ceremony is necessary for marriage to obtain its civil effect, there would be no complaint from the Church, of course. As for public worship, it must be carried out entirely in the interior of the church edifice (Art. 24), a peculiarly vexatious restriction in a country with Catholic and Latin traditions. Moreover, even in the interior, worship is subject to the intervention and supervision of the civil authorities (Articles 24 and 130).

Education is declared to be free (Art. 3), a remnant of the former Constitution; in spite of this, however, religious education is forbidden in all primary schools, even in private ones, and these are subject to Government authority, not only in matters of hygiene, safety, etc., but also in curriculum, number and quality of instructors, and so on. The power of conducting primary schools is absolutely denied to religious bodies, while no institution of higher learning conducted by a religious group can have any official recognition for academic degrees or credits (Article 3, 130).

It is forbidden for any periodical or news-paper which can be considered sectarian by its programme, its title or its ordinary tendencies, to make any comment on national political affairs (Art. 130), even when these latter concern denial of fundamental rights.

All church edifices are declared to be the property of the Nation, and the Federal Government can convert them to other uses (Art. 27), while new ones can be erected only by authorization of the Secretary of the Interior, and they in turn become property of the State (Art. 130). The churches are likewise to be deprived of ownership of Bishops' houses, parish houses, seminaries, asylums, colleges, convents, and all institutions of private benevolence (Art. 27). A clergyman becomes incapable of inheriting any property, except from his immediate relations (Art. 130), and the Church may exercise no ownership over real estate or the income from real estate (Art. 27).

For infraction of the provisions of Article 130, which, as will have been noticed, is the principal one in this matter, no one may enjoy the right of trial by jury.

From the years 1917 to 1926, this part of the Constitution remained inoperative, since no Enabling Act had been passed, and no penalties imposed, and though many extra-legal vexations were suffered, there was relative peace. In the latter year, however, President Calles, who had succeeded General Obregon in 1924, took steps to remedy this defect. On January 7, Congress handed over to the Executive extraordinary powers to make legislation by Presidential decree. On June 14, the decree on religious infractions was signed, and it was promulgated on July 2, to take effect July 31.

This decree-law imposes heavy fines and imprisonments on those who violate the above-mentioned provisions of the religious legislation. It expels all foreign clergymen; it dissolves all monasteries and convents; it forbids anyone to wear any garb, or badge, even the Roman collar, distinctive of a clerical calling; it proceeds to the immediate confiscation without indemnity of all church edifices, parish houses, schools, colleges, hospitals, etc., and their conversion into public buildings; for purposes of its prohibitions, it defines clergymen as all who give religious instruction to anyone, even in private, and it defines as religious bodies all pious associations for religious purposes, even without vows; and it punishes anyone who should presume to criticize acts of the Government, even of local mayors.

Previous to this, the Government had already set as a condition of being allowed to exercise the priestly ministry, the duty of inscription in the municipal register, and it had severely reduced the number of priests allowed in each State. Thus in the State of Jalisco, with 1,000,000 Catholics, only 250 priests were allowed; in Oaxaca, with the same population, only 30; and in my own diocese, Tabasco, only five priests were allowed, and then only on condition that they marry, which effectually expelled the Church from that State.

Probably the best way to help Americans to visualize the state of things such legislation has brought about in Mexico, is to suggest what effect it would have if it were passed in the United States. By decree of the President, not by an Act of Congress, such organizations as the Anti-Saloon League, the Methodist Board of Temperance, Prohibition and Public Morals, and the Federal Council of Churches, would be suppressed; no clergyman, Protestant or Catholic, would be allowed to vote in any election; all private primary schools would be closed; foundations, such as that of Trinity Church, in New York, would be confiscated; periodicals, like the various *Christian Advocates,* would be restricted to printing strictly religious news and editorial opinions; all parish residences and annexes would be confiscated; and, by the same ratio to population, ninety per cent of the clergymen in the country would be expelled from the ministry.

This comparison, however, was not necessary for the readers of this REVIEW to understand why Church leaders in Mexico resisted this legislation. The spirit in which it was conceived is clear enough; it was designed to render it impossible for the Church to carry on. In fact, practically every means at the usual disposal of religion is taken from it: the ministry of the priest is converted into an agency of government, with every inducement to the weak and unfaithful to go into schism; the training of the priest is made impossible, with seminary schooling suppressed; the recruiting of educated men to the priesthood is checkmated, since Catholic colleges are deprived of scholastic standing, and hence must die out; no missionaries may be brought in from abroad, while the training of little ones in parish schools, which experience shows is the great bulwark of sturdy faith and future religious practice, is stopped entirely. . . .

Shortly after the restrictive regulations went into effect, the dispute, as usually happens in such cases, crystallized in the public mind around one point, and one which, perhaps, is not so easily explained to the American mind. It concerned the inscription of the priests in the local municipal register, as a condition of their being allowed to continue their ministry. If this measure had been designed merely as a census operation, there would probably have arisen no objection. Both sides, however, understood it as much more than this. For one thing, it was a preliminary to a wholly unjustifiable limitation of clergymen at the will of the local authorities. But even more than this, there entered in the question of principle, so dear to the Latin mind and so much more important to it than mere external legal forms. This registration was undoubtedly intended by the Calles Government as a sign and symbol of subjection of the Church to the State in purely spiritual matters, and the acceptance of it as an act of surrender, and still further, of secession from the Catholic Church. Anyone who doubts this may read the debates of the Constitutional Convention on Article 130. The answer of the Church to the declared will of Calles to enforce the will of the Convention was the closing of the churches, but not — and be it sharply noted — as a purely political gesture to bring

Calles to terms, but as a measure of compulsion, to avoid continuing them in circumstances which would have been tantamount to secession from Catholic unity, which in the eyes of all Catholics would be gravely sinful. This fact was undoubtedly known to Calles when he took this initiative.

Apart from this question of principle, however, I think I have said enough to indicate that the purpose of the religious legislation of the Social Revolutionary party in Mexico was a blow aimed not particularly at the Catholic Church, but at all religion impartially. About the execution of the legislation I have purposely refrained from speaking. Suffice it to say that it has been done with extreme brutality, more than fifty priests to my personal knowledge having been killed in a year, after a mock courtmartial, or, more often, no trial at all.

In every case, their crime was to have attempted to continue their priestly ministry. In some cases their good name was even taken away from them along with their life, for they were falsely accused of having taken part in revolutionary activities against the Government, and forged confessions were not unusual.

In closing, I would like to return to my first words. The philosophy which animates the anti-religious legislation in Mexico is as much opposed to American political ideals as it is to Catholic principles, and is in fact the source, on the Mexican side, of all the difficulties which have arisen between the countries. Moreover, that same philosophy is being constantly spread through Latin America and constitutes a menace that cannot be ignored by any lover of peace or good government.

The Church Has Suppressed Religious Liberties

JAMES CANNON, JR.

In July 1926, the very month when Calles of Mexico promulgated a series of anticlerical laws severely restricting clerical and religious activities, Current History published a series of articles dealing with the Church-State problem; both clerical and anticlerical views were expressed. James Cannon, Jr. was a Methodist Bishop who had little sympathy for the plight of the Catholic Church in Mexico.

THE two outstanding deliverances concerning the present relationship of Church and State in Mexico are the Apostolic letter from Pope Pius XI, the final authority of the Roman Catholic Church, to the Archbishop of Mexico, and the statement by President Calles, the head of civil authority in Mexico. The Apostolic letter bears the date of Feb. 2, 1926, although it was not

made public in Rome until April 19. The statement of President Calles was issued in Mexico City on Feb. 24 and published in the press of the United States and Mexico on the following day.

The Apostolic letter denounces in strong, bitter terms the present Government, statute laws, and even the Constitution of Mexico.

From James Cannon, Jr., Current History, Vol. XXIV, No. 4 (July 1926), pp. 491–495, 498–500. Reprinted by permission of the publisher, Current History.

The latter part of the Apostolic letter *"is an especial advice and command"* that the bishops develop "united Catholic action." What is meant by "united Catholic action" is not clearly defined, for while the Apostolic letter declares that "all Catholics of the Republic of Mexico are forbidden, as such, to establish any political party under the name of Catholic," and while, "above all, bishops and priests, in keeping with *their praiseworthy record of the past,* must not become members of any political party, nor write for the journals of any political faction," the letter in the following paragraph emphatically declares that

the faithful . . . cannot be forbidden to exercise those civic rights and duties which they have in common with all other citizens. In fact, their very faith and the common welfare of religion and country require that they make the best use of such rights and duties. Even the clergy cannot refrain altogether from an interest in civic affairs, or put aside completely all care and solicitude for the things of public life. Indeed, although holding themselves studiously aloof from any attachment to any party, they ought in keeping with their priestly office, and safeguarding the sacredness of their ministry, to promote the welfare of their country by diligent and religious exercise of their civil rights and duties, and by setting a good example which the faithful can follow so that each one of them will studiously comply with their public obligations as the laws of God and the Church demand.

Certainly if the Apostolic letter has any meaning it is a positive command by the Pope for "united action" in civic affairs by the Roman Catholics of Mexico.

THE CHURCH'S RECORD

It must be agreed that, if they are taken apart from their historical setting, some of the laws referred to in the Apostolic letter are unusual and drastic. But that very fact compels a careful examination of the reasons therefor.

The Roman Catholic hierarchy, controlled entirely by the foreign priesthood, not only did not aid the movement to secure better conditions for the Mexican people, but encouraged, if it did not initiate, the reactionary movements under Iturbide and Santa Ana, and openly, with desperation, fought Juárez and all his reform laws. Finally, when Juárez realized that there could be no free government in Mexico until clerical interference and domination were overthrown and incorporated in the Constitution of 1857 the epoch-making provisions stripping the Church of its ill-gotten wealth and abolishing religious orders, convents and monasteries, the Vatican itself, as today, joined in the conflict and was an active participant in the conspiracy to place the Habsburg Archduke Maximilian upon the throne of Mexico as Emperor, and the Roman Catholic hierarchy in Mexico were Maximilian's most ardent supporters.

BANCROFT'S TESTIMONY

When Juárez returned to power after the execution of Maximilian and during the term of office of President [Lerdo de] Tejada and the earlier years of President Díaz's Administration, the ecclesiastical laws were upheld fairly well. Under the protection of the Constitution, beginning about 1870, despite continued and bitter Roman Catholic opposition, several Protestant churches began mission work in Mexico, numerous schools were opened, a higher educational standard was set, and illiteracy was cut down to about 80 per cent. The rule of General Díaz, however, gradually assumed the form of a dictatorship; the Government was carried on in the interest of a small minority, and the Roman Catholic hierarchy, under the leadership of its foreign priesthood, under the patronage of Señora Díaz, gradually crept back into a position of privilege and power. Although the Constitution of 1857 had nationalized all of the then existing Church property, the laws of 1874 permitted the Church to acquire and to hold properties necessary to carry on its work, and this privilege had been taken advantage of by the Church to the extreme limit, President Díaz raising no objection.

When Madero and his followers started the revolution of 1911 to secure more freedom and better living conditions for the people, the Roman Catholic leaders opposed it, and after the assassination of Madero supported the usurper Huerta until his overthrow by Carranza. It was this continuous "record" — not "praiseworthy," as Pope Pius asserts, but shameful — of the active hostility of the clergy to the republican form of government for over a hundred years, and the efforts of the clergy to use its tremendous power over the ignorant, superstitious people, and to teach the children in the schools that the Government was not approved by the Pope and therefore must be opposed by all faithful Catholics that impelled the framers of the present Constitution to add to the provisions of 1857 the more drastic provisions of 1917.

To rid the country of the domination or influence of foreign priests who have too often been simply parasites, the law declares that only a Mexican by birth can exercise the ministry in Mexico, and it gives to the State the authority to determine the number of ministers permitted to exercise the ministry in any State. No religious body or minister of any religious sect is allowed to establish or direct schools for primary education; no member of religious orders can wear a garb indicative of his calling; no religious ceremonies can be held anywhere except in church buildings. Ministers are forbidden to criticize the civil laws or authorities, to vote, to hold office or to participate in assemblies for religious purposes. Periodical publications of a religious character may not comment on political affairs. No meeting of a political character may be held in the churches. Marriage is a civil contract, although a religious ceremony may follow. . . .

RELIGIOUS EXERCISES UNHAMPERED

The purpose of the Mexican Government has not been and is not today to prevent anyone from preaching or from giving religious instruction to children. It has not attempted to prevent the Church from controlling whatever amount of property is necessary for its *legitimate spiritual* activities. The purpose of the Mexican Constitution is not to limit in any way the spiritual activities of the Church. The great purpose of the Constitution, of the laws and regulations and of the Government of Mexico is to uproot clericalism, to prevent forever the accumulation by the Church of unnecessary wealth, and particularly to prevent the participation in political activities and domination of the Government by the Church and especially by the foreign priesthood.

Within the past few days (May 29) Bishop Zarate has been tried for issuing a pastoral letter denouncing certain clauses of the Mexican Constitution. This is a direct violation of the Constitution, which forbids all ministers of religion to criticize the laws or officials of the country. The Apostolic letter was an "advice and a command" to Bishop Zarate and all the Mexican bishops to do what the Constitution of the country forbids them to do. He made his choice and decided to obey the Pope and to defy the Constitution and the Government. This is doubtless the action which the Pope expected and desired to follow from the Apostolic letter.

President Calles's letter appeared on Feb. 24. It dealt specifically with the expulsion of foreign priests and the closing of primary schools which were conducted by priests or clergy or nuns, or in which religious instruction was being given. After calling attention to provisions of the Mexican Constitution on these two points President Calles declared:

The foreign priests whose presence in Mexico is no longer being tolerated had received warnings on various occasions from the Department of the Interior to cease exercising their ministry and dedicate themselves to some other activity if they were desirous of remaining in this country. Without paying any attention to these notifications the priests to whom I refer continued exercising their ministry in violation of Article 130 of the Constitution. In addition almost all of them were violating Article 3, which provides "that no religious corporation or minister of any cult will be permitted to establish or superintend primary schools."

REASONS FOR DISCRIMINATION

In stressing the fact that there has been no religious persecution of any church or any sentiment of animosity toward any foreigner, President Calles frankly states in clear-cut language the reason for the discriminations made by the Mexican Government between the activities of the foreign Roman Catholic clergy and the foreign ministers of other cults:

In contrast to the attitude of the expelled priests there have been numerous ministers of other cults who have obeyed the constitutional provisions. They have dedicated themselves to other legal activities, such as teaching in secondary schools or to orienting or superintending suitable activities of their church, but without exercising their office in ritualistic acts and leaving to the Mexican ministers the performance of the strictly confessional work of their religion. These ministers have not been and will not be molested. . . . Almost without exception the American ministers of confessional churches which are not Catholic adjust themselves while residing in Mexico to what the law demands. For this reason they are not molested, thus bringing about development and prosperity of their churches through the work of Mexican ministers, and living tranquilly and respected among us, merely performing acts of religion.

It will be noted that President Calles makes a clear-cut distinction between "ritualistic acts" and "the strictly confessional work of their religion" on the one hand, and "merely performing acts of religion" on the other, and this distinction is justified from a political viewpoint. . . . The Mexican Constitution does not forbid the performance of "ritualistic acts" by Mexicans, but only by foreign priests, holding that experience has demonstrated that this discrimination is justifiable; that while foreign priests will be dominated entirely by the Vatican and think of Mexico simply as a province of the Church, as in the past, the Mexican priests will be so influenced by love of country and the views of their friends and kindred that they will prefer to cooperate with the Government in its efforts to develop the country and advance the prosperity and enlightenment of the people.

Mexico Is a Godless State

WILLIAM FRANKLIN SANDS

Diplomat and author, as well as active Catholic layman, William Franklin Sands was one of three distinguished men to be sent to Mexico by the American Committee on Religious Rights and Minorities; the commission was requested to determine the extent to which religious liberties, and indeed organized religion itself, had been broadened or destroyed as a result of the Mexican government's actions. On his return from Mexico, Sands wrote a series of articles for *The Monitor*, the official organ of the Archdiocese of San Francisco; these articles were then published as a small book entitled *The Present Condition of the Church in Mexico*. The following selection is included because of its measured tone.

FRANCISCO MADERO

WHEN Francisco Madero undertook to overthrow Díaz, many of the great landowners were sympathetic to him and to the theory of agrarian reform. Several times during Díaz' rule the leading Catholics, clerical and lay, had attempted reforms of that same general character, only to be discouraged by the Government. It is not the new reform program that has been opposed by Catholics, as the revolutionary propagandists now assert before American audiences, but the manner in which it has been put into practice: ineptly, half fanatical, half cynically corrupt.

From 1910 to 1917 all the released forces of disorder swept Mexico into complete ruin. From 1917 a new small group of hard and masterful men emerged in control of the Revolution, first as rivals, then as a triumvirate, and of these Calles alone has survived. Practically all the others met violent death in one form or another.

One way to consolidate the beginnings of a new era and to tie in loose ends, was to organize the National Revolutionary Party and to discipline it. Calles accomplished that in such a way as to preserve for a time the necessary "anti-reactionary" and Radical tone. When the Party developed its definitely anti-religious rather than anti-clerical trend as its principal tenet, Catholics who had sympathized with Madero and the Revolution ranged themselves in armed opposition to it. In Mexico it is as difficult as it is elsewhere to conduct an armed revolt upon delicate and refined lines. Even though "Christ the King" was inscribed upon the new banners of a revolution against the Revolution it takes hard fighting men in addition to idealists to make a revolt successful. In the uprisings from 1926 on unpleasant things were not confined to the government side. Many things occurred on the "Cristero" side also which are adduced by Government today in justification of "regulatory" and "control" measures alleged to be necessary to keep a "rebellious and seditious clergy" in order. Foreigners who study that phase of Mexican history generally overlook the fact that neither side was fighting daintily. Mexicans, kindly and courteous and gentle as they are in normal life, are serious fighters when they are aroused — and fight to win.

From William Franklin Sands, *The Present Condition of the Church in Mexico* (Washington: Saint Matthews Book Stall, 1935), pp. 11–16.

It is still argued passionately in Mexico that the "Cristero" revolution was on the point of success and the National Revolutionary Party on the point of collapse, when "the American government" intervened through Dwight Morrow "to uphold the Calles regime." It is generally omitted from discussion of that point, that the Vatican also was not favorable to Civil War. Many Mexicans still deplore the accord that was reached at that time with Calles, promulgated by the new President, Portes Gil — and never carried out, once the Cristero bands had submitted and turned in their weapons to the Government.

The result of that surrender has been a split in the Mexican Catholic body itself. Some of the bishops, clergy and laity favor peaceful solution, hopeless as that may seem. Some favor renewal of armed rebellion against imposition upon Mexico of the new Godless State, which is in process of evolution there. These latter are kept under close supervision by the National Revolutionary Party, whose spokesmen assert that these "rebellious" Mexican Catholics are being secretly aided financially by American Catholics — and find in that assertion ample warrant for future persecution. The rift between Mexican Catholics themselves obviously adds difficulty to their internal situation and makes more than difficult any proper approach by American Catholics to aid them in their solution of the problem. . . .

CALLES AND CÁRDENAS

General Lázaro Cárdenas, President of Mexico, was put in office by Plutarco Elías Calles. Like his immediate predecessors he was put there to carry out Calles' ideas and not to have any of his own. In June he advanced certain very definite ideas of his own, in defiance of Calles, and the Dictator submitted and left Mexico. It is still a question whether the quarrel was real or "framed"; whether Calles, wishing to retire, allowed Cárdenas to show himself to be big enough to defy him (in order to discourage other competitors for the Presidency) or whether Calles was deceived by Cárdenas' Indian stolidity into believing him to be the silent, docile, faithful satellite he appeared to be during all the Cristero campaign.

Cárdenas is a good type of the new Mexican. He is a young man, grown to maturity during the complete revolutionary chaos of 1910 to 1929. He has no education outside of the technical military school. It is probable that he has never had personal contact with religion, nor with a bishop, priest or nun, except as outlaws. He has a high reputation for personal integrity and honesty. Some credit him with considerable native shrewdness. Others give him no credit whatever for ability outside of his military profession.

To him the Revolution would be, in all probability a very real and noble thing, exposed as he has been all his life, to the revolutionary condemnation of everything that went before. The program of the National Revolutionary Party for the uplift of labour, of the agricultural Indian, and for "practical" education, would seem (as they truly are, if properly understood) most desirable.

CALLES' WARNING

Calles' warning against radical excesses may well have seemed to Cárdenas to be something sacrilegious.

All that is very easily intelligible. There is no doubt that Mexico, an agricultural nation entering an industrial stage of development, has every duty to avoid the injustices and abuses which have flawed and vitiated the whole economic life of all the so-called progressive countries. There is no doubt whatever that the gradual social development of the great mass of Indians who form the bulk of the population is a problem of the utmost magnitude — and a most difficult one to solve within the forms of Constitutional Democracy. There is equally no doubt that the program of public education should be directed to those two objectives, and it might well contemplate a process of "de-fanaticization" in religious matters, properly understood. Superstition is not a part of Catholic life. It is an abuse. It is widespread in Mexico. It is in many ways a natural consequence of the long struggle in Mexico, within the Church itself, for spiritual autonomy.

Cárdenas took a leading part in supressing the Cristero uprising. He is perfectly aware of the fact that it was a Catholic movement "against the Government" — the first government approaching stability which he had seen in all his life. He was aware that while motivated by idealism and religious zeal the Cristero bands also contained fighting elements as ruthlessly cruel as his own men (as would be perfectly natural in Mexico) — and that priests accompanied many of these bands as chaplains, or even, in case of necessity, as fighting men or guerrilla leaders. It would seem quite natural to him, in all probability, to keep them down now, by every means short of persecution, since they are, to him, enemies of the only social order he knows. He would be skeptical of this unknown quantity of religion as a spiritual and social force. He has never seen it that way, in the turbulent years of his manhood. To that kind of mental attitude the recent pastoral letter of the Mexican bishops was obviously the right approach, though it is difficult to see, at the present stage of affairs, whether it will have a beneficial effect, or merely be set down as a political move. Cárdenas is not necessarily to be classified as a persecutor of the Church. He is a new type. . . .

ANALYSIS NECESSARY

The actual Church-State situation in Mexico is a deadlock. The Catholic hierarchy has not yet worked out a complete and harmonious program. Their recent Pastoral Letter is a long step in that direction.

It is difficult to go further effectively since there is no suffrage; only members of the National Revolutionary Party may vote. Yet quiet persistence not force, nor war, is what the Pope wants and has recommended to them.

While the National Revolutionary Party is growing into a new and tangible thing, it is true that three public characters still dominate the horizon: Calles, Cárdenas and Portes Gil.

A REAL DILEMMA

Calles knows that while there is much in the new program of social reform that is both necessary and good, it cannot be fully accomplished as long as this deadlock exists. He realizes that it is not desirable to repeat the error of Porfirio Díaz (though in the opposite direction) and to draw into the Mexican problem of a guided evolution of Indian peoples to a culture of their own, all the current postwar European (or Asiatic and African) ideologies, which do not fit the Mexican situation. Undoubtedly he knows also that the Party has come to that point to which all revolutions must come, when to recede from an ultra-radical position is perilous — and equally perilous not to recede.

Cárdenas, as has been said, is a completely new man, grown to maturity during the twenty-five years of revolutionary ruin and chaos — totally unfamiliar with anything that went before, or with anything outside his military profession.

INTEGRITY OF CÁRDENAS

The honesty and integrity with which he embraces what seems to him to be a new order of things, may be the very rock upon which any effort at conciliation may founder. Cárdenas cannot possibly be aware that his Party's school program is not a new order of education, but only a sweeping up for Mexican consumption of all the European crumbs of "inevitable conflict" between Science and Religion of eighty-five years ago, when it seemed necessary to choose between the two. To demonstrate to him compatibility rather than conflict between Science and Religion, or to show him the possibility of harmonizing both in education, would probably take a longer time than any Mexican President can reasonably expect to retain his high office.

. . . The Catholic Church is totally incompatible with that kind of a State in which religion is abolished, or subordinated to the State. That is the kind of State which is beginning to evolve in Mexico. It is of all forms the one that used to be most feared and abhorred by all Americans. It is the negation of everything basic in American institutions. It is true that it finds support in America today in many of our leading universities. On the other hand, it is equally true that a formidable number of Americans still believe in our fundamental principles in that regard and are ready to stand together wherever they recognize the issue clearly.

III. AGRARIAN REFORM

Agrarian Reform Is Prolonging Poverty

W. W. CUMBERLAND

In July 1935, the University of Virginia Institute of Public Affairs sponsored a round table discussion on the Mexican Revolution. Three United States' citizens—two Catholic clergymen and a distinguished economist, Dr. W. W. Cumberland—were invited to participate as critics of the Mexican government.

REVOLUTIONS are traditionally so popular in Mexico that the party in power continues to call itself the Revolutionary Party, although twenty-five years have elapsed since the particular revolution was launched of which the present administration is the lineal descendant. Few countries in recent years have had governments which made greater protestations as to solicitude for workers and farmers. Yet the condition of the population, in comparison with available natural resources, does not convince the detached student that governmental control of the country's economic life by a so-called revolutionary party is synonymous with public welfare.

In Mexico, as in Russia, the "revolution" has never represented public opinion. A useful analysis of the present situation in Mexico should therefore dissociate itself from word-mongering and not attempt to classify the Mexican government as liberal, revolutionary, or communist, but merely subject its policies to the tests of actual and prospective achievements. Let us try to know the facts, and then apply the same reasoning and judgments as for other countries. . . .

From a legal point of view, the basis of the fourth phase of Mexican agricultural history is found in Article 27 of the Mexican Constitution of 1917. This article declares that title to all land resides in the state and that the Mexican citizen, by reason of his status as such, has a right to land for his necessary use. Two methods were adopted of giving effect to this right. First, land formerly in the possession of village communities or those which had been taken by force or fraud from individuals was to be restored. Second, sufficient additional land was to be obtained from large estates to provide small plots for the landless. The first method is known as restitution, and the second as dotation or donation.

Many persons believe that ownership of private property, particularly land, has been abolished in Mexico. This is not the case. Conditional ownership has merely been substituted for unrestricted, perhaps irresponsible ownership. While title to land, water and subsoil resources is declared to be vested in the state, exclusive possession of lands and certain waters may be granted to private persons. Not only are substantial land holdings continued for existing owners as a matter of law under the Constitution of 1917, but individual distribution of cultivable lands is required of such parcels as have been made available to the landless

From W. W. Cumberland, *Economic and Social Program of Mexico* (Mexico, 1935), pp. 50–82.

through the process of restitution or dotation. Common ownership is in force only for certain urban zones, pasture land and wood land and for necessary water rights. During the early years of application of the present agrarian policy, numerous categories of individuals and villages were disqualified from obtaining land under Article 27 of the Constitution.

At present there are few disqualifications of actual peasants and agricultural laborers from obtaining land, but continued ownership by the person to whom land has been given is circumscribed, and his disposition of the land while ownership continues is not unrestricted. For example, possession is valid only by reason of productive use. Failure of the owner to cultivate his property results in its reversion to the community. Nor can the individual lease, rent, mortgage or alienate his plot. On the other hand, it passes to his heirs at his death, provided they continue cultivation.

Scant consideration in introducing the present agricultural policy in Mexico has been given to existing landholders, so far as protection of their wealth in land is concerned. These landholders, or their ancestors, showed equally small compunction in the acquisition of their holdings. But the process of assembling the great states, as well as the method of their dismemberment, demonstrates the fundamental lack of devotion to orderly processes which has for centuries prevailed in Mexico and which is a principal cause of the unsatisfactory progress which that country has made. Shocking abuses can be acknowledged in the formation and operation of the latifundias without justifying the equal disregard of orderly procedure in exercizing the right of public domain which has been so extensively employed as the predominant characteristic of the present agrarian policy.

Since the latifundias had not vindicated themselves by social, economic, and political results, a fundamental change in basic land policy was clearly required. But it should have been accomplished in a manner to encourage enterprise and thrift, rather than

in one to increase existing doubt as to the value of those virtues when practiced in Mexico. . . .

In essaying to determine the results achieved under the agrarian policy the chief obstacle is lack of information. Mexican statistics are notoriously inadequate and unreliable. It is a characteristic of the Mexican temperament that plans, laws, decrees, administrative commissions and other paraphernalia in regard to the agrarian program are available in abundance, but that little real information can be found in regard to how all of this elaborate machinery works out in practice. In a literal sense the agrarian program is largely a paper structure, if not an air castle. . . .

Our credulity is taxed when we are asked to believe that 353,750,000 acres are devoted to farming purposes, as such an area constitutes more than 75 per cent of the entire territory of Mexico. Even a casual journey in Mexico demonstrates that only a minor portion of the land is used for farming. Vast regions cannot possibly be farmed, due to ruggedness, lack of rainfall or other causes. Hence the statistics of land devoted to farming have to be discarded as erroneous, and grave doubt is also cast upon the statistics of distribution of farms in accordance with size. . . .

Taking Mexican statistics at their face value, it is found that land utilized for farming purposes amounts to approximately 19.9 acres per capita, as compared with 3.4 acres per capita in the United States. Obviously, this simply is not the case. If the land utilized for farming purposes as shown by the Statesman's Year-Book is accepted, land actually farmed per capita is 1.5 acres per capita, as compared with 3.4 acres in the United States. This computation at least seems to correspond with known facts.

From the establishment of the policy of land restitution and dotation to the end of June, 1930, the National Agrarian Commission of Mexico estimates that 8,995 villages had applied for land, out of a total of 25,854 which under the laws then in force had a right to make application.

Thus only a little more than one-third of the villages were sufficiently interested to make the effort necessary to participate in the agrarian program. Of the villages making application, 3,877 had definitely been granted land, and the petitions of 1,176 had been denied. Land actually granted to villages amounted to 16,860,000 acres, or 3.4 per cent of the area of the Republic. This land was taken from 6,993 properties and constituted 13.4 per cent of the area of such properties. Needless to say, the better portions of these properties were expropriated, consisting of 19 per cent of their cultivated areas, 36.7 per cent of their forest land, 12.6 per cent of their pastures and 5.1 per cent of their mountain land. The Commission estimated that 13,000 villages will ultimately receive additional land in the amount of 23,502,500 acres. Under this assumption, 40,362,500 acres or 8.2 per cent of the area of the Republic will eventually be included in the ejidos or communal undertakings.

From the initiation of the land distribution program to the middle of 1931, according to Mexican official reports, land had been awarded to 773,819 families. These families are estimated as constituting some 20 per cent of the total of the Republic and an even larger percentage of rural families. Land plots distributed to each family averaged 22 acres. A considerable proportion of the plots is not susceptible of intensive cultivation. Portions of the good land are not well cultivated. Observers in general agree that the lands thus far distributed have not afforded and possibly are not capable of affording a satisfactory standard of living to the families which have received them.

Of the areas distributed to peasants to December 31, 1931, 3,250,000 acres or 20 per cent were obtained through restitution of lands adjudicated as having been improperly taken from villages or individual peasants, while 13,250,000 acres or 80 per cent were acquired through the simple process of expropriating private land from medium-sized to large estates, virtually without compensation. Under the terms of the latest revision of the agrarian program, agricultural plots to be distributed to farmers are supposed to amount to ten acres for "land that has sufficient water for the customary crops of the region or receive sufficient moisture through rainfall or by any other means," and to twenty acres for unwatered or inadequately watered land. Compared with the average size farm in the United States of 157 acres, either of these areas appears to be too small to support a prosperous population.

According to the Mexican Ministry of Foreign Relations, 4,400,000 acres were awarded to 119,000 heads of families from February to November, inclusive, of 1934. Estimates by the Mexican Department of Agriculture are that a total of some 900,000 grants of land had been made from the origination of the program to July, 1934, and that there are some 1,600,000 to 2,000,000 persons who are entitled to receive grants of land under existing legislation.

On the basis of these estimates the land distribution program may be considered as approximately one-half accomplished.

Per capita income in Mexico was calculated at $36.00 per annum in 1929, as compared with $657 in the United States. Such incomplete statistics as are available indicate that the chief crops in Mexico have declined somewhat during recent years, with the result that annual income is probably no higher in Mexico than it was in 1929. Yet local and foreign observers seem to share the opinion that the agricultural worker and the inhabitant of the rural village have bettered their condition during that period. This is impossible to prove or disprove. Possibly the answer is to be found in definite improvement of education and a small start toward road construction, while the peasant continues to live, eat and react much as he has done ever since the conquest. . . .

In its agrarian aspects the Six-Year-Plan[1]

---

[1] The plan under which Cárdenas was to operate during his 1934–1940 term. [Editor's note.]

contemplates an amplification of Article 27 of the Constitution, together with the necessary laws and decrees for putting the broadened provisions of the Constitution into effect. It extends but does not essentially change the agrarian objectives and methods which have with greater or less intensity been pursued since the adoption of the Constitution of 1917. In general, the laws of earlier years relating to land distribution are codified, and the short-comings of law and administration developed by experience are supposed to be removed. . . .

For giving effect to these purposes the plan provides for much recasting of administrative organizations and methods, renewed activity in the restitution of communal lands and the division of large private estates, colonization projects and redistribution of rural populations, assistance to Mexican farmers in improving the cultivation of their lands and marketing their products, and financial support for all of the foregoing policies and activities.

This far-reaching program largely represents aspirations and objectives and only to a minor degree has it yet been put into practice. . . .

Under an amendment of the Mexican Constitution, dated December 30, 1933, it was provided that owners of land which was taken under the agrarian dotation progress should be indemnified by receiving three per cent bonds of the Mexican Government. These bonds carry no date of maturity and no amortization fund, and are quoted locally at some seven per cent of face value. Moreover, valuation of land for purposes of compensation is to be identical with its declared value for tax purposes. Since landholders under the old regime had controlled the machinery of government, it was notorious that land was carried on the tax rolls for a fraction of its value. There may be a certain amount of ironic justice in hoisting landholders by their own petards. Nevertheless, the practical fact remains that destruction of property rights forms no solid foundation upon which to erect a sound economic structure in Mexico, a structure which will in time provide a decent standard of living for the mass of the population.

Authoritative statements cannot be made as to whether the land policies of the Madero revolution and succeeding revolutions have aided or impeded progress of the Mexican farmer and agricultural laborer toward an improved condition. Following on the Madero revolt against Díaz came a long struggle for power in Mexico, with no single leader in unquestioned control, with the exception of former president Calles. Economic unsettlement caused by the war and post-war periods was superimposed on the disruption caused by internal revolution. At about the time that Mexico might have been in a position to demonstrate the merits, or lack of them, of its economic innovations the depression arrived to disturb economic calculations and to make impossible fair appraisals as to the effects of the agrarian and labor policies in improving the welfare of the Mexican population. Although as an essentially agricultural country Mexico did not feel the impact of the depression as acutely as was the case in industrial countries, it was sufficiently affected to require suspended judgment in regard to the social value of its labor and agricultural programs.

No one knows what the condition of the Mexican peasants would have been under a different policy. No one knows what it would have been under the existing policy in the absence of prolonged periods of political unsettlement and a world-wide economic depression. And the existing condition is one of widespread poverty, illiteracy, political inadequacy and an unsatisfactory standard of living.

Commendable efforts are being made to extend irrigation. A systematic program to provide needed irrigation was inaugurated in 1926. Since that date water is stated to have been furnished to 737,500 acres, at a cost of $24,547,000. On these irrigated lands 14,674 colonists have been placed, who are farming 437,500 acres. This is a creditable performance, and plans for further extending irrigation works have been made. For 1935 approximatetly $2,775,000 has been appropriated for this purpose.

Considerable prominence has been given to the financial support to be accorded by the Mexican government to irrigation and to the extension of rural credit. When it is discovered, however, that total credits to be provided by the National Bank of Agricultural Credit under the Six-Year-Plan amount to $13,900,000, with $5,560,000 to be available during 1935, and that total actual and proposed expenditures on irrigation amount to some $50,000,000, the small scope of the plan is apparent. As a corollary, the time when adequate capital for agricultural improvements will be available is necessarily extended into the distant and indefinite future. This conclusion is further emphasized by inquiry into the amount of banking capital in Mexico.

In 1926 a National Bank of Agricultural Credit was established. From that date through 1933 loans to agricultural cooperatives and local agricultural societies were made in the sum of $3,098,000. Loans to individuals amounted to $9,096,000. Thus the total was $12,194,000. At the end of 1933 outstanding loans were $1,205,000, in the case of agricultural societies and $1,265,-000, in the case of individuals, or a total of $2,470,000 for the entire Republic. These aggregate figures are less than the loans of each one of thousands of small banks in the United States. Needless to say, the amount of financing by the Mexican Agricultural Bank during the entire period, as well as that afloat at the end of the period, was merely nominal in comparison with the needs of the country.

Under the Six-Year-Plan the National Bank for Agricultural Credit proposes, as stated above, to make total loans of $13,-900,000 for financing peasant farmers. Such a trifling figure merely shows that the pretensions of the plan cannot be realized because of inadequate funds. It is also a commentary on the utter deficiency of domestic capital for financing a broad agricultural program. Nor is capital from abroad likely to make itself available, as the entire experience of foreign capital in Mexico since the revolution of 1910 has been highly unfavorable. . . .

To Americans, the most interesting feature of the Mexican Six-Year-Plan is its resemblance to our own New Deal. A pervasive officialdom is involved. Few economic activities are outside of the purview of government. Individuals are no longer expected to think for themselves but to do as they are told. Outstanding enterprise and thrift are not to be rewarded. Property is not to be protected. Contracts are to be observed if convenient. Foreigners are to have little or no part in developing the resources of the country and are to be subjected to special discriminations. Governmentally supported efforts are to be made for setting class against class. Currency policy and banking technique which have resulted in material progress wherever applied are to be abandoned and supplanted by methods which have been synonymous with economic stagnation.

Like the United States, Mexico has a complete right to adopt economic policies which result in poverty for the population and which disregard the country's responsibilities as a member of the family of nations. Personal liberty, orderly government and material prosperity may be of less importance than the privilege of obeying instructions from bureaucrats. Political and social equality derived from communal ownership of land may be a greater good than sanitary plumbing, automobiles, radios and expensive educational facilities. Promises of Utopia are certainly more alluring than the harsh capitalistic philosophy of hard work and thrift as a means of obtaining a high standard of living. Mexico has made its choice, and the United States is headed in the same direction. Social values under the Mexican Six-Year-Plan may be high, but the standard of living will remain low.

Agrarian Reform Is Beneficial

RAMÓN BETETA

Dr. Ramón Beteta was then and later intimately involved in the planning and the administration of various economic developments. He was asked to sustain the position of the Mexican government regarding past actions and future planning before the same round table discussion. A portion of Dr. Beteta's remarks were in rebuttal to points made by Dr. Cumberland.

I SHALL not go into the details of the background of the Mexican Agrarian Reform. There are two points, however, which I shall mention. First, one must try to understand what the deprivation of their lands meant to the Mexican natives. It was not only an economic blow. Psychologically it was more than that. It was condemning them to exile, depriving them of their fatherland, tearing them away from the origin of all power and all life; land, a very real God!

To say that Mexico has been conquered more than one time, is not a metaphor. The "moving of the land marks"; the "denuncios" of the surveying and colonizing companies; the "punishing" by the Federal troops of supposed rebellious tribes and all the various other means by which the natives were forced to abandon their fields and work as "peons" for the *hacendados* have been so many deeds of conquest which, from the standpoint of the Indians, cannot be distinguished from the arrival of Cortez to the fertile Valley of Tenochtitlán.

The second point I want to inist upon is the fact that the "hacienda" system of land holding is not only unjust, as it creates peonage which is slavery without legal protection; harmful, as it breeds political abuse; damaging to the country, because it forms an absentee ownership; but besides all this it is a very primitive, backward, inefficient method of production. Agronomically the "hacienda" which cultivates

solely the best part of the land, which uses no system of crop rotation, which employs no artificial fertilizers, which has no equipment besides a few oxen and some wooden plows, represents the middle-age method of agricultural production. It is a system of manpower and land instead of machinery and natural resources.

Few people question today in Mexico the justification or the necessity of the Agrarian Reform. Even the *hacendados* have already accepted the desirability of changing the old system of land holding. The discussion has reduced itself to the method rather than to the principles.

The law of January 6, 1915 which was later incorporated into the Constitution of 1917 provided three systems of land distribution; restitution, donation and ampliation. The first takes place in those cases in which the Indian villages could prove that they had been illegally deprived of their lands. The second is outright donation and follows solely the principle of necessity: all communities needing land have the right to receive it. Finally, ampliation is a new donation to those communities not having sufficient land in spite of previous grants. Following all of these three methods land has been distributed in Mexico with a speed which varies with the zeal of the President of the Republic in the agrarian question because his decision is indispensable in every case.

During the first five years the Agrarian

From Ramón Beteta, *Economic and Social Program of Mexico* (Mexico, 1935), pp. 22–46, 86–94.

Reform took practically only the form of restitution, and in fact, very few hectares of land were distributed. One may really say that the Agrarian Reform begins in Mexico in 1920. During the Presidency of General Obregón it got well under way and within the following term, that of General Calles, a steady increase in distribution of the land is to be noted. During the ad-interim Government of Portes Gil, more land was distributed than during the four years of his predecessor, although his term lasted only fourteen months. Then comes the Government of Ortiz Rubio, during which the Agrarian movement slowed down, and it was even in danger of collapse. The provisional Presidency of General Rodríguez, in spite of the fact that many people thought he was rather conservative, was also fruitful in dividing the land.

President Cárdenas, well known for his enthusiasm in regard to the Agrarian Reform has given new stimulus to the move-ment. In one single day, May 1, 1935, to celebrate Labor Day and the Chicago inci-dent,[1] 552,936 hectares of land were dis-tributed to 353 villages and to the benefit of 36,856 heads of families.

The latest and the most reliable statistical figures we have representing the movement are due to the Agrarian Census taken last April 10. The preliminary results of such census show that there were in Mexico 7041 "ejidos," (we call an *ejido* a village which has received land from the Govern-ment by any one of the three methods already mentioned) benefiting 895,284 heads of families who have received 11,-741,191 hectares of land, of which 3,735,-931.14 hectares are crop land. The rest is considered as pasture or as wood land, not suited for cultivation.

This gives a rough idea of the extent of the Reform, so far as the actual distribution of the land is concerned. One must remem-ber, however, to really understand its sig-nificance, that Mexico has only 14,517,699 hectares of cultivable land and that accord-ing to the Census of 1930, 3,626,278 per-sons were gainfully employed in agriculture.

It is important in this connection to insist once more upon the necessity of being aware of the fallacy of Mexico's unlimited wealth. In fact, it is the scarcity of arable land that has made the Agrarian Reform so acute. As you know, Mexico is a moun-tainous country with insufficient rainfall and therefore a large part of its territory is unfit for agricultural purposes.

That considerable progress has been made, however, is shown not only by the figures given above, but also by the tre-mendous change in the attitude of the people. One cannot judge the Agrarian Reform in terms of economic factors alone. The Mexican people are the children of their land where they have lived for cen-turies; where they have multiplied and grown; where they resisted the incursion of the Spaniards, the dryness of the desert, the awe of the mountain and the sterility of the jungle. Attachment to the soil is the central factor in the psychology of our people. Having back their lands our native popula-tion are again in harmony with nature.

There is one point which always comes to one's mind in connection with the pres-ent-day situation of the Agrarian Reform in Mexico: the productivity of the "ejido." Visitors of Mexico have often asked me whether or not it is true that the agricul-tural production has steadily decreased as the distribution of the land has progressed. This unfortunately is a question that can-not be answered categorically, as there is a complete lack of information of the pre-revolutionary period. An accurate compari-son between the pre-revolutionary and the post-revolutionary periods is especially diffi-cult to make, because there has been a change of crops and consequently, while there is a decrease in certain crops, there has been a considerable increase in some others. Besides, as many of the rural com-munities of Mexico are practically self-sufficient and produce for consumption pur-poses only, as they live practically in a pre-pecuniary economy, it is very difficult to

[1] The Haymarket affair, May 1886. [Editor's note.]

calculate the production even through indirect means. We may, however, attempt to get an approximate idea by the comparison of importation statistics. If we take the period 1901–1907 as typical of the Díaz Regime, and we compare it with that of 1929–1934, as an example of the post-revolutionary period, we find that corn, flour, meats, dairy products and cotton, among others, were imported in larger amounts during the period of 1901–1907 than in the second.

The more significant of these products is corn, because that is the most important crop of the Republic, both in the extension of land under cultivation and in the volume of the crop. And yet, there was not one year, even in the most prosperous times of our octavian peace, in which Mexico did not have to import some corn. The same thing could be said about beans, our second most important crop. On the other hand, during 1934 and the first months of this year, Mexico has been exporting both corn and beans in comparatively large amounts.

In 1934, Mexico exported 71,079 tons of corn, and during the first four months of 1935, 65,117 tons. For beans the figures are: In 1934, 12,205 tons, and for the four months of 1935, 4,428 tons.

Those figures seem to indicate that there has not been a decrease in agricultural production. But there is still another way to prove it. The Agricultural Census of 1930 tells us that while the "haciendas" cultivated 48.27% of their crop-lands, the "ejidos" had under cultivation 57.35% of their crop-land. This is especially remarkable in view of the inferiority of the agricultural equipment on the part of the latter.

The question of agricultural production resolves itself in the last analysis into one of the standard of living of the Mexican people. But here again, we have no way to make any accurate comparison. There have been a few studies made in this respect. One of them made by the Department of Statistics last year, a special study of 300 families of the working class in the Federal District, shows the incredibly low standard of living of our industrial workmen, and we have good reason to believe that the situation in the rural districts is still worse. But low as it is, our standard of living today is higher than it was before the Revolution as even a superficial observer cannot fail to see.

But as the leaders of the movement soon realized, the Agrarian Movement to be successful cannot be limited to land distribution. Credit and education are just as essential. To solve the first question, the Agricultural Bank was created in 1926 with fifty million pesos capital, of which the Federal Government contributed with twenty million pesos, seven of which were given in properties, and the rest in cash. The bank soon found itself in a difficult situation due to the duality of its function. On the one hand, it was supposed to organize the "ejidatarios" into cooperatives and to operate with them with no purpose of making profits, and on the other, it was to make loans to small, and even large, landowners seeking a commercial profit. Naturally, as it needed a large personnel to organize and supervise the co-operative societies, its overhead was altogether too heavy for a commercial bank, and at the same time it used a great deal of its capital in large loans to big "hacendados." For this reason the National Agricultural Bank was accordingly re-organized in 1931 to operate exclusively with the "ejidatarios" organized in cooperative societies, and had been operating that way with success since that year, until 1934 in which it was fused with what remained of the other experiment in rural credit — the Regional Banks.

Nine of these banks had been founded in various States of the Republic and each suffered from two main handicaps: the lack of capital (each was supposed to have 200,000.00 pesos, but on the average had about a hundred thousand pesos) and the inevitable intermixing of politics which made their functioning very difficult during the four and a half years in which the system was in operation. This explains why the two systems merged into one. . . .

In spite of the many difficulties which it had still to encounter due especially to the inability of the Federal Government to contribute with the amounts promised, the system improved during the following years, until that of 1934 when a new law permitted the bank to operate with small or middle size farmers, provided that loans be guaranteed by mortgages and that no private individual receive a loan of more than 25,000 pesos whatever may be the value of the property. Besides, the loans to private individuals must always be made at a rate of interest not less than two points higher than that prevailing for the least favored institution.

There are some other minor changes which the law of January, 1934, introduces into the system. Especially the possibility for the Bank to operate with Societies of Collective Interest, which are non-profit making and may not extend credits to individual members. These societies are temporary organizations which may obtain credit for specific purposes, such as the building of irrigation or drainage, works of electrification, industrialization, etc.

The most important point however, in connection with the system of agricultural credit is to be found in the Six-Year-Plan, which states that in the six years covered by it, the Government will invest without fail the sum of fifty million pesos in Agricultural Credit, of which the first twenty million must be contributed precisely in the year 1934.

If one compares the number of ejidatarios and their financial need with the possibilities of the National Bank of Agriculture and the associated banks, one must realize how far we are from solving this problem. At the same time, knowing the peculiarities of the question, the lack of experience on the part of the ejidatarios, the complete absence of any capital, the special sort of rights that they have on their land, (the impossibility of mortgaging or alienating the ejido parcels) one comes to the conclusion that more than a problem of banking, one is confronted with an educational question.

If what has been done is significant, it is not on account of the comparatively small amount of capital used for agricultural credit, but due to the attempt to visualize the system as a part of a more complex question, that of educating the rural masses and preparing them to grow out of the non-pecuniary economy in which they live into a co-operative system, which will make it possible for Mexico to improve the standard of living of its population without having to plunge itself blindly into capitalistic regime. . . .

What has been said only proved that Mexico neither in fact nor in theory has accepted a communistic organization even in the most advanced of its revolutionary reforms; the Agrarian Movement. It is true that there is a tendency at the present time to speed up the distribution of the land as shown by the creation of the autonomous Agrarian Department and the various laws and regulations which aim at doing away with red-tape in the procedure of land granting. It remains true, however, that the attitude of the Government is that of respect for the right of private property.

Not everybody, however, accepts this view. There is a group that considers this attitude ill-advised. Not only the history of Mexico, at least in the central and southern States, shows that the holding and the working of the land in common is feasible, but also the history of the United States and Europe is a warning against the individualistic type of economy, which does not seem to have succeeded in creating a stable, acceptable, economic system which would bring the greatest happiness to the greatest number. Much to the contrary, the present efforts of the American Government to regulate agricultural production, the enormous difficulties it is facing, and its very limited success, are good arguments against repeating in Mexico the history of her neighbor to the North.

Some of us in Mexico have visualized differently the future of agricultural economy. We believe that Mexico finds herself in a privileged position to determine her destiny. By being in a pre-capitalistic state with some of her people even in a pre-pecuniary economy and at the same time by observing the effects of the last crisis of the capitalistic world, we think that we should be able to use the advantages of the industrial era without having to suffer from its well-known short-comings. We think that we should attempt to industrialize Mexico consciously, intelligently avoiding the avoidable evils of industrialism, such as urbanism, exploitation of man by man, production for sale instead of production for the satisfaction of human needs, economic insecurity, waste, shabby goods and the mechanization of the workmen. This is not an impossible dream. We are convinced that the evils of capitalism are not to be found in the application of machinery to the productive process, but rather are due to a merely legal question: who is the owner of the machinery. We want the land and its necessary equipment to be at the disposal of those who till it, rather than be the means of exploiting these men. Some of us believe, furthermore, that profit making is not the only incentive of human endeavour, but rather a motive that happens to have been chosen and over-developed in the capitalistic regime.

There is nothing fatal in the mistakes of the system, or at least so we hope. We have dreamt a Mexico of "ejidos" and small industrial communities, electrified, with sanitation, in which goods will be produced for the purpose of satisfying the needs of the people; in which machinery will be employed to relieve man from heavy toil, and not for so-called over-production. In these communities machine-made goods may still be beautiful for they will be made by the same people whose artistic sense is now expressed by the work of their hands, and there is no reason to believe that the changing of the tools will *per se* make them

different. What mechanizes men is not the use of machinery, it is the pressure brought to bear upon them to produce at the highest speed the largest amount possible.

In short, we have chosen the "ejido" as the center of our rural economy. Within its limits "land belongs to him who works it with his hands" as our Indian poet expressed it. New methods of production, machinery and new technique will be introduced without having to make rugged individualists out of the ejidatarios and at the same time without killing the human desire of progress in those communities. Then, and only then, could national economy be planned, not by directing the conflicting interests of the various individuals, but by conceiving the country as a unit whose needs are to be satisfied by the harmonious working of these villages, agricultural or industrial, in an effort to make the whole country secure and prosperous.

* * *

If the conditions of our population in comparison with our available natural resources are not good, that does not prove the failure of governmental control on economic life, it proves solely that a heritage of four hundred years of misgovernment could not be amended in two and a half decades. To blame the Revolution for the low standard of living of our laboring classes means to forget that the Revolution is to be explained precisely as a revolt against those conditions and against a system that made them possible and permanent.

I am prompt to admit that the way in which millions of people live in Mexico is nothing to be proud of, but why blame the Revolution which is aware of such a situation and is anxious to help it, instead of putting the blame where it belongs: in the system which was responsible for the "scientific" government of Mexico based precisely on the principle that the exploitation of the working classes was necessary, moral and for the good of the country? On the other hand, let me call your attention again to the fact that our available natural resources are by no means as great as it is generally believed and that they have never been in the hands of the Mexicans or exploited for their benefit. . . .

Anyone familiar with the procedure followed in the distribution of land in Mexico, knows that one of the main reasons why the process has been so slow, is because of the desire to give the land owners every opportunity to defend themselves. It was with this idea in mind that the Law provided for a second hearing in every case. It is my personal opinion that the excess of protection is responsible for the slow pace of our Agrarian Reform. The only point in which one could imagine the existence of "scant consideration to the landholders" is in the system followed to valuate the land. And yet, here Mr. Cumberland has to admit that the landholders found themselves in a very ironical position, for no one could think that any government should accept one value on land to collect taxes, and another to pay for that land when expropriated. . . .

To demonstrate that Mexican statistics are notoriously inadequate and unreliable, Dr. Cumberland chooses to use figures which are wrong *but not given by the official organ of the Mexican Government*. In our official publication one may read that the amount of arable land in the country is estimated around fourteen million hectares or about thirty-five million acres. The figure used by Dr. Cumberland, 353,750,000 acres, is simply wrong and there is no need to waste any time proving it. From the use of wrong figures, however, one could not conclude the inadequacy of Mexican statistics, but only the lack of care of the one using them indiscriminately.

In distributing land in Mexico the principle of necessity was followed. Any village lacking land is entitled to receive it. In other words, the Government does not interpret the need of land, but waits until the village expresses it. This unfortunately puts the greatest stress on the weakest link of the chain: the village, which often is subject to all sorts of manipulations on the part of the landlords to keep the people from filing a petition for land. Thus, it is not fair to say that only a little more than one third of the villages of the country were "sufficiently interested" in 1930, to ask for land. What one should say is that the rest were unable to do likewise on account of the various pressures brought to bear upon them. . . .

In discussing the Agricultural Bank, Dr. Cumberland informs us that its capital is inadequate. I am ready to admit it, but one should not attempt to compare its resources with those of the banks in the United States, or with the budget of the American Federal Government, but rather with the possibilities of Mexico. In order to give our National Bank of Agriculture twenty million pesos the Federal Government must use almost one tenth of the whole of its budget. The idea of pretending to obtain foreign capital for our Bank of Agricultural Credit is absurd, for it is not operated as a profit making enterprise, but rather as part of the Agrarian Reform and as an important aid to the National Educational Program. . . .

There is a similarity, it is true, between the New Deal on the one hand, and the Mexican Six-Year-Plan, on the other, as they both are efforts at harmony in planning the economic chaos produced by economic liberty. There are, however, fundamental differences between the American and the Mexican approach to the problem. Thus while the aim of the United States Government, as I understand it, is to increase the prices by limiting production and make profits possible, we in Mexico are more concerned with the worker's side of the problem than with the industrial's. We recognize the existence of class struggle as one of the inevitable features of capitalism and we have put our sympathy with the working class. Realizing that poverty cannot be decreased by diminishing production, we do not want to follow that line of approach, but rather we desire an increase in production which will be brought about by the improvement of technique but which will not make production an end in itself. On the contrary, we want production for the satisfaction of the needs of the people engaged in creating it.

Finally, in the mind of Cumberland, political and social equality excludes such things as sanitary plumbing, radios, and educational facilities. But that is not the case, in fact, we are convinced that those material improvements could not be obtained except through social equality.

Agrarian Reform Has Brought Democracy and Increased Production

CLARENCE SENIOR

Clarence Senior, who has practiced his profession as sociologist in both academic and nonacademic positions, has been intrigued with the agrarian program almost from its inception; the Laguna District, with its collectivized *ejidos* has been of special interest to him. He first visited the Laguna area in early 1937, a few months after President Cárdenas had distributed nearly a million and a half acres of land to thirty thousand peasant families in the vicinity of Torreón. Not long thereafter he published a short and optimistic account of the experiment. About twenty years later he returned to make a more lengthy study; in the intervening years he had lost none of his optimism although he had perhaps become more critical. The following excerpts come from his chapter entitled "Democracy Comes to a Cotton Kingdom"; he is primarily concerned with the development of democratic institutions.

THE "reconquest of Mexico" by the Mexican people actually began seriously with the revolution and in many respects the revolution actually started with Lázaro Cárdenas. More vigorous, widespread, and fundamental attacks were made on the colonial and feudal heritage under Cárdenas than under any other revolutionary president. That many parts of that heritage are still extant should surprise no one who is aware of the persistence of outmoded cultural traits even in more dynamic societies. Their persistence among relatively static peasant groups is readily understandable.

. . . It must be remembered that the Mexican Revolution began seven years before the Russian and that the 1917 Constitution was adopted eight months before the October "ten days that shook the world."

One of the greatest causes for misunderstanding of modern Mexico by her northern neighbor has been her different attitude toward land tenure. The tradition of land being held in fee simple, dominant in the United States, is contained in neither the Indian nor the Spanish parts of the Mexican heritage.

The Indian and Spanish heritage holds as queer and antisocial the doctrine that land can be bought and sold as can a sack of flour. Land is the property of the community, for the use of members of the community so long as they follow the socially-fixed rules for its use. This is a concept to

From *Land Reform and Democracy* by Clarence Senior. Published by the University of Florida Press, 1958, pp. 184–205. Used by permission.

which many cultures give their sanction. Even Great Britain, the home of Adam Smith and the classical seat of laissez-faire, swung around to a similar position in the prolabor government Uthwatt reports and in the Agricultural Act of 1947. The greater part of Australia's land area is publicly owned and the majority of her farmers hold leases rather than titles.

There are those in our own culture who wonder whether the complete power to "use and abuse" land does not contribute to antisocial behavior and result in losses rather than gains to the economy. Restrictions on this right have been adopted piecemeal for many years. They have yet to be given an adequate, well-rounded public expression in policy. Scholars and publicists sound an alarm, however. An outstanding student of land problems states: Private enterprise in the ownership, use and exploitation of most natural resources has not been justified by its results. One of the tasks facing our government during the next century will be to repair the ravages resulting from three centuries of waste and spoilage under private enterprise.

The impact of capitalist ideas from the north, particularly during the Díaz regime, threatened the ancient Indian and Spanish heritage, but did not destroy it. The revolution had rubble to clear away in the field of land law, but no fundamental reconstruction. It had no such good fortune in the field of civic attitudes, however. The Laguna experiment would have been difficult enough in Switzerland, Denmark, Sweden, or any other land where democracy has historic roots and where there is a tradition of widespread participation in political life, solidly based on years of popular education and almost universal literacy. Mexico, instead, is still struggling to overcome the colonial heritage mentioned above. . . . Old institutions were destroyed insofar as their legal bases were involved. Since institutions are, in the last analysis, only viable when they are buttressed by the values which are meaningful to the people, let us now turn to an assessment of the Laguna experiment in terms of the goal values of democracy adopted from Lasswell's study.

Power — The monopoly of power once held by the small *hacendado* class in the Laguna region has been broken. Legally, the *ejidatario* now has a voice and a vote not only in political matters but also in complex economic decisions. He participates in decisions as to the crops he is to raise, the price and time of sale of his products, the use or nonuse of machinery, the distribution of water, and even the election of the "field-boss" who is to supervise his daily labor. He owns, jointly with the others of his ejido, the land on which he works and often sizable quantities of farm machinery. His and other ejidos jointly own electric power plants, cotton gins, and other capital equipment.

He belongs to the peasants' organization and in its meetings debates its policies. He and his wife and children now have schooling available; they travel as freely as their economic circumstances permit.

The *ejidatario* no longer must make his purchases at the hacienda store; he can shop in the community store or he can join his friends and drive the *ejidal* truck to the most convenient urban market, or to a cooperative store. His participation in social life, his status in society, the role he plays, all have changed in the direction of the sharing of power and a voice in the making of decisions.

The ejido itself has become the basic element in what is legally among the most fundamentally democratic political and social structures in the world. Its constitution provides for "checks and balances," for minority representation and protection. The personnel in charge of the crucial economic function of the direction of production is subject to the democratic process. Turnover of elected officials depends on the will of the majority in the ejido.

The "field-boss" no longer is appointed by an outsider, one who might even be considered an enemy of the land worker. The writer has attended many elections of ejido officials. He was accompanied at two by the president of the Farmers' Union of a midwestern state. "If I had one-tenth of my membership able to conduct meetings in such a responsible manner and participate with such wisdom," said the official after the second meeting, "I would have the most important farmers' organization in the United States." The writer has been similarly impressed at the overwhelming majority of the meetings he attended.

Not all ejido meetings are conducted in such a responsible manner, however. Cliques have developed around personalities, or ejidos have divided politically along family lines. Some elected work-chiefs have used demagogic slogans to gain reelection; some rivals have used similar tactics to displace a successful man who applied discipline against a popular member. Such hazards of any democratic political system are particularly important in an ejido since the economic welfare of the entire group is involved. . . .

Wealth — Both increased production and more equitable distribution of economic goods and services are subsumed under this goal value heading. "Land reform which does not increase production merely equalizes poverty," Chiang Mon-lin, chairman of the Joint Commission on Rural Reconstruction in Formosa, points out. Production of cotton and wheat has increased in the Laguna region since the expropriations. The increase, ironically enough, has come mostly from the private properties. Their owners have been forced to intensify cultivation, using wells and machinery to a higher degree than before.

Productivity, the basic factor in real income, has risen for the private sector of the Laguna economy but, on average, has fallen for the *ejidal* sector. The total production of both cotton and wheat increased after the expropriations by 14 and 52 per cent, respectively, as we have seen. Yields fell, however, from an average of 396 kilograms of cotton per *hectárea* in the six years just before the change to 339 in the following ten years and from 1.19 metric tons of wheat to 1.14. Tables 20 and 21 show that the drop was greater in *ejidal* than in

TABLE 20

COTTON: AREA CULTIVATED, PRODUCTION, AND YIELD
PRIVATE PROPERTIES AND EJIDOS
LAGUNA REGION
1936–1937 TO 1945–1946 (*crop years*)

CROP YEAR	AREA *Hectáreas*		PRODUCTION BALES OF 507 LBS.		YIELD KGS. PER *Hectárea*	
	EJIDOS	PRIVATE	EJIDOS	PRIVATE	EJIDOS	PRIVATE
1936–1937	90,944	29,056	84,649	55,351	214	439
1937–1938	66,472	26,198	94,000	53,000	326	466
1938–1939	56,329	28,971	65,000	68,000	266	541
1939–1940	50,589	23,319	55,016	50,000	251	494
1940–1941	37,753	55,984	50,000	70,846	305	292
1941–1942	50,016	70,000	64,921	139,010	299	457
1942–1943	56,699	71,881	95,445	166,843	388	535
1943–1944	61,538	78,777	55,000	132,500	206	387
1944–1945	41,606	60,805	84,737	99,757	469	378
1945–1946	23,312	28,257	33,816	56,514	334	461

Source: Compiled from reports issued by: Secretaría de Agricultura; Banco Nacional de Crédito Ejidal; Departamento Agrario; Banco de México, Torreón office; Pequeña Propiedad Agrícola de la Comarca Lagunera, A. C.

private production and that the latter exceeds the former in almost every year in both crops.

Our examination of the reasons for these phenomena must begin with a qualification of the accuracy of the figures. Reporting of

TABLE 21

WHEAT: AREA CULTIVATED, PRODUCTION, AND YIELD
PRIVATE PROPERTIES AND EJIDOS
LAGUNA REGION
1936–1937 TO 1945–1946 (*crop years*)

CROP YEAR	AREA *Hectáreas*		PRODUCTION METRIC TONS		YIELD METRIC TONS PER *Hect.*	
	EJIDOS	PRIVATE	EJIDOS	PRIVATE	EJIDOS	PRIVATE
1936–1937	7,093	19,407	7,835	21,616	1.10	1.11
1937–1938	33,329	19,024	37,452	29,487	1.12	1.55
1938–1939	51,136	18,364	53,000	32,000	1.04	1.74
1939–1940	39,401	19,620	54,683	35,317	1.39	1.80
1940–1941	43,278	14,500	47,957	16,000	1.11	1.10
1941–1942	55,420	15,000	41,479	15,000	.75	1.00
1942–1943	30,485	10,000	34,126	12,000	1.12	1.20
1943–1944	21,664	12,000	20,094	15,000	.93	1.25
1944–1945	33,991	23,051	32,999	46,955	.97	2.04
1945–1946	20,453	11,463	13,205	12,800	.65	1.12

Source: Compiled from reports issued by: Secretaría de Agricultura; Banco Nacional de Crédito Ejidal; Departamento Agrario; Banco de México, Torreón office; Pequeña Propiedad Agrícola de la Comarca Lagunera, A. C.

agricultural data in the region, as elsewhere in Mexico, leaves much to be desired. Essentially, the figures are those provided by the interested parties; the *ejidal* by the Banco Ejidal and the private by the owners. The totals of some years exceed the crop figures of the federal agricultural department and in other years drop below it. The *ejidal* figures are published and subject to challenge, however, while the others are not. In all cases of discrepancy between what seem to be equally reliable sources, the more conservative figure was accepted.

Analysis of the causes for the difference in yields must of course take into account all the factors which influence production: the quality of the soil, water supply and timing, that is, river flows, rain, and wells; weather, application of labor to the land, that is, management efficiency; mechanization, and credit. Unfortunately, in the

region, another factor must be included — cotton theft. Obviously cotton stolen from *ejidal* lands and sold as if raised on the private properties not only reduces the yield records of the ejidos but increases it on the private properties and thus counts double in any comparative figures. Theft of wheat is far less prevalent than that of cotton and therefore would be a minor factor in comparing yields. Cotton yields dropped noticeably more than wheat yields.

Wells are an important factor in water supply. . . . Both cotton and wheat yields are raised substantially by irrigation with well water, which can be timed exactly to suit the crop needs. The private owners now have 65 per cent of the wells in the region for 30 per cent of the land.

The fertility of the soil obviously plays an extremely important role in production. There are no soil maps nor analyses of private as compared with *ejidal* lands, but it will be recalled that the *hacendado* was free to choose at least 150 *hectáreas* (370 a.) of his holdings. Obviously he generally would choose the most fertile soil. It may reasonably be assumed therefore, that the private lands contain the choice soils of at least the zones in which they are located. . . . The amount remaining under one management is often considerably more than 370 acres. The private farmer has the advantage of unified direction of a larger area. He does not cut his land into plots to be worked by families. The private owner has a completely "collectivized" farm, but of course run under a more or less modified dictatorship, not a democratic collective. It may or may not be more efficient than a farm run by a committee. One finds a wide range of overlapping between the efficiency curves of private farms and ejidos, with some ejidos ranking above some private farms and vice versa.

The relative position varies widely by zone and by crop, as indicated in Table 22, which takes the average private property yields in cotton and wheat for the year 1945–1946 as a basis for comparison between the two systems.

A crucial factor in modern farming is mechanization. Other factors being equal, a well-mechanized farm will far outstrip a nonmechanized or poorly mechanized farm. It has been seen above that the returns are appreciably higher on the heavily mechanized ejidos. It has also been seen that whereas 75 per cent of the private properties were heavily mechanized in 1939, only 23 per cent of the ejidos were. The influence this fact has on yields has been reported.

Inadequate credit completes the picture.

TABLE 22

YIELDS, WHEAT AND COTTON

COMPARISON OF EJIDAL WITH PRIVATE PROPERTY

LA LAGUNA 1945–1946

(per cent of all ejidos in relation to average private property yield)

ZONE	WHEAT			COTTON		
	ABOVE AVERAGE	SAME AS AVERAGE	BELOW AVERAGE	ABOVE AVERAGE	SAME AS AVERAGE	BELOW AVERAGE
1	27.8	33.3	38.9	—	—	100.00
2	18.2	13.6	68.2	—	9.1	90.9
3	50.0	16.7	33.3	4.2	8.3	87.5
4	34.8	17.4	47.8	4.3	—	95.7
5	13.3	3.3	83.4	3.3	3.3	93.4
6	8.9	11.1	80.0	—	—	100.00
7	37.1	14.3	48.6	2.9	—	97.1
8	65.0	—	35.0	20.0	5.0	75.0
9	55.2	6.9	37.9	3.4	—	96.6
10	—	—	100.0	—	—	100.00
11	48.7	9.8	41.5	12.5	10.0	77.5
12	33.3	13.3	53.4	20.0	6.7	73.3
13	16.7	4.2	79.1	8.3	—	91.7
14	9.1	9.1	81.8	—	10.0	90.0

Source: Compiled from reports issued by: Secretaría de Agricultura; Banco Nacional de Crédito Ejidal; Departamento Agrario; Banco de México, Torreón office; Pequeña Propiedad
Source: Compiled from reports issued by: Secretaría de Agricultura; Banco Nacional de

The private owner generally may be able to get credit fairly quickly and simply since he can mortgage his property, although even he is hampered by the general lack of farm credit facilities in the country as a whole. Government credit suffers from a complicated bureaucratic system of so many checks that as much as six months may pass from the application date before money is available to an ejido.

"Lack of discipline among the membership" and many other factors are often stressed as causing the difference in productivity between the private properties and the ejidos. This would lead to the conclusion that the *ejidal* form of organization is the reason for the difference in yield, even though we have pointed out other factors which reasonably can be linked with the observed differentials.

Indications of greater economic welfare . . . include better housing and clothing, more beds, radios, group possession of capital equipment, garden plots, domestic fowl and animals and horses. La Laguna cannot be separated economically from the rest of Mexico, however. Relatively more prosperous than the country as a whole, it still suffers from the raging inflation of recent years, from the general overpopulation of the country in addition to its own specific population problem, from the dislocations of unplanned and uncoordinated economic development, and the interference of self-serving politicians in regional economic matters.

Well-Being — It is toward this goal value that the Laguna experiment has made the most progress. Much of the advance is now past quantifying. One thinks, for example, of numerous reports of eye-witnesses and participants in whippings of field workers only a few months before the expropriations; of houses destroyed and peons driven off haciendas only a few years before 1936. One remembers hundreds of meetings in which men and women vibrated with a new dignity and determination to work hard and make a success of the "land which is now ours." One recalls the mixed meetings of

ejidatarios, private owners, urban businessmen, and government officials into which the former day-workers came armed with facts and figures, presenting well-reasoned arguments for their position with calmness and determination. One rereads the annual reports of the old Central Union in which a recommendation was made that a mutual crop insurance fund be created, and follows this through the years to the present thriving organization which could well serve as a model for farmers in other nations.

It is possible roughly to quantify one crucial index to the feeling of security which has been won by the *ejidatarios* of La Laguna. On the writer's first visit to the region, March, 1937, a count of all peasants visiting the Torreón office of the Banco Ejidal showed nine out of ten wearing at least one revolver, supported by a well-loaded cartridge belt; there were many "two-gun" men! Each succeeding visit found a decreasing number of guns. All had disappeared by 1939. A gun-carrying official of the bank was encountered in 1943; a surprised query brought this response from a peasant leader: "He has just been transferred here from Jalisco and he hasn't got used to our ways yet!"

The reply indicated a glaring difference between the region and many other sections of Mexico where frequent *despistolización* campaigns have been conducted intermittently ever since the writer's first trip to the country in December, 1936. The Mexican is still "quick on the draw," although an improvement may be noted between 1940 and 1954. There were 13,175 homicides registered in the former year, to 10,954 in the latter, in spite of a substantial increase in the population in that period. The rate dropped from 66 per 100,000 to 38. That was still the highest rate reported by the United Nations for 1954.

Skill — It is in this area of values that one of the most interesting changes has occurred among the *ejidatarios*. Almost all the skilled personnel in the region before the expropriations worked for the *hacendados*. The more highly skilled ate at the table of the landowner, swam and played golf at the country club, and gambled at the casino. They were naturally lumped with the *hacendados* as "enemies of the peasant." The peasant had no skills, no reason for having skills, and no opportunity to acquire them if he wished. The sons and daughters of the peasants were in the same situation.

The expropriation gave rise to a tremendous demand for skilled and semiskilled persons. A new attitude was needed, as well as new facilities for acquiring skills. The latter were furnished quite promptly. . . . Changing attitudes was somewhat more difficult. There was a fairly widespread disposition to repeat the same naive democratic shibboleths so often encountered in the United States in past times: "Any good man is capable of filling any good job — and I am the man." The presence of a corps of agrarian technicians in the entourage of Lázaro Cárdenas helped overcome that attitude as land was being distributed.

The world suddenly became a much more complex phenomenon than it had been. Bookkeepers, water gagers, cotton classifiers, mechanics, electricians, well-tenders, drivers, and even economists and lawyers were needed to help the new landowners find their way along strange and untrod paths.

Now . . . the *ejidatarios* either do these jobs for themselves or hire those who know how to do them. Their experience has taught them the value of skills and through the public educational system both regional and national, they are able to acquire those they need.

One of the great handicaps to Mexican progress until the past two decades has been the paucity of adequate facilities for training competent technicians, especially in the agrarian and agricultural fields. . . . Simpson pointed out in 1937 that:

the Mexican student who actually goes out in the field and looks for facts about his own country is so rare as to be a curiosity. I could name on the fingers of one hand the research monographs dealing with modern Mexican social problems published by Mexican students in the last decade which by any stretch of the imagination could be called scientific.

Considerable strides have been made toward remedying that situation, as is shown by the well-grounded scholarly current output of scientific monographs and of articles in such journals as *Cuadernos Americanos, Investigación Económica, Problemas Agrícolas e Industriales de México, Revista de Economía, Revista Mexicana de Sociología,* and *El Trimestre Económico* and in the progress since 1943 of the Comisión de Fomento de Investigaciones Científicas under the direction of the world-famous atomic physicist, Dr. Manuel Sandoval Vallarta.

Shared Enlightenment — Information and interpretation available to the most remote reaches of the region, the smallest and the largest ejido, to the poorest and the best endowed was part of the original frontal attack on the heritage of feudalism.

Much has been done. Schools now mark each ejido (one has two within fifty feet of each other because of the rivalry between the directors of the Coahuila state department of education and the federal organization!). However, the education of the *ejidatarios* themselves in a manner designed to involve them in "problem-solving" has been neglected in a most irresponsible manner. There are several reasons for this. First, the drive for education was supplied initially by the Cárdenas administration. When it went out of office the key post of secretary of education was occupied by a political appointee whose chief qualification seemed to be a hatred of democratic ideas. The regional education office was abolished and a wet blanket was thrown over the enthusiasm of both teachers and inspectors. Second, an economy wave hit the Banco Ejidal, resulting in the discontinuance of the *Boletín Ejidal* and the weekly educational broadcasts. Third, a "commercial" orientation was adopted by the bank. Seemingly it was oblivious to the fact that its clients could not make a complete transition in a few years from virtual slaves to self-reliant members of a far-reaching democracy. Fourth, employees of the bank who either did not share the democratic ideals for which the institution was supposed to work or who wanted to capitalize on the ignorance of the *ejidatarios* often did not carry out even those plans which were authorized.

Mexico as a whole and the region in particular have partially made up for this situation, however. The almost universal aspiration for education and information has resulted in the proliferation of sources of news and discussion of public issues in the daily press, in magazines, and on the radio. The country in 1954 counted 127 dailies and 1,128 magazines, most of them weeklies, compared with 60 dailies and 159 magazines in 1935. The circulation of periodicals of all types doubled between 1930 and 1954.

Furthermore, individuals of standing and ability have for some years felt free to criticize governmental policies and can depend on most organs of mass communication to give circulation to their statements. The revolution, as a matter of fact, is officially represented by only one inadequately-staffed daily newspaper in the capital and one radio station; the "opposition" has all the other hundreds of outlets for "news and views." Also, there is an old tradition of "wall newspapers" and handbills which comment on public affairs.

Shared Affection and Respect —Lasswell defines the former expression as meaning the acceptance in the culture of "the desirability of congenial human relationships." Here we find in La Laguna and other parts of Mexico, many expressions of such revolutionary slogans of human brotherhood as solidarity of the worker and peasant. The feelings extend even to "workers and peasants" throughout the world, delegates and "fraternal visitors" from other groups and other countries are welcomed cordially at labor union and peasant conventions. Many times real friendships grow out of contacts made in working for "the common cause." This would seem marginal to the major patterns, however. Actually, it is in this goal value that Lasswell's schema seems least applicable to the Mexican culture, unless one confines the word "congenial" to its root meaning of "kindred."

Mexico has been in a state of social disruption so often and so much of the time for the past four centuries that the family (biological and ritual) is almost the only place in which a man can "let down his guard." Expression of pleasant and sympathetic feelings towards persons outside the family do not seem to be as common as in the United States, except among the small but growing urban middle class.

Much has been made of the key role of the family in the Mexican culture by social scientists and journalists, both foreign and domestic. Unfortunately, the vast majority of Mexican ethnographic studies treat of relatively isolated rural or village "folk." However, some of the aspects of family structure and function are fairly widespread. Most observers seem to agree with Redfield that "there is no open conflict within the family," that the father wields undisputed authority, that submission is the role of the other members, that the family plays a vital role in economic and political life, especially in small villages.

Lewis reports on "the quality of interpersonal relations" in Tepoztlán as follows:

There is a readiness to view people as potentially dangerous, and the most characteristic initial reaction to others is suspicion and distrust. Lack of trust is not only present among non-relatives but also exists within families and affects the relations of husbands and wives, parents and children, and brothers and sisters. This is not a neurotic distrust, but one rooted in the hard realities of Tepoztecan social and economic life, in patterns of child training, and in a long history of conquest, colonial status, and internal and external political and economic exploitation. In Tepoztlán, the motives of everyone are suspected, from the highest public officials of the nation, to the local priest, and even to close relatives. It is assumed that anyone in a position of power will use it to his own advantage at the expense of others. Honest government or leadership is considered an impossibility, altruism is not understood. The frank, direct person, if he exists anywhere in Tepoztlán, is considered naive or the greatest rogue of all, so powerful or shameless as to have no need to conceal his deeds or thoughts. An individual who is obliging without cost to those who seek his aid is understood to have some as yet unrevealed plan for capitalizing on his position.

The greater degree of social participation among the peasants of La Laguna seems to have eliminated some of the traits reported from other areas of Mexico, if it may be assumed that they were once present due to a common cultural tradition. For instance, cordiality and hospitality of the Laguna *ejidatarios* to the writer and his colleagues of the American Friends Service Committee and the college students from "north of the border" many times have been embarrassingly fulsome.

The same acceptance was never achieved with the Torreón middle class. Many business and professional people grudgingly expressed their interest to the writer, but usually ended by regretting that the students "couldn't see the *real* life of the Mexicans instead of living and working with those peasants." The consular representatives of the United States in Torreón in the early days of the work-camp program invariably were critical of it on the ground that it "impaired the dignity of the American" in the eyes of the only Mexicans their staff knew — the urban middle class.

These experiences might indicate that as changes of the kind experienced in recent years in La Laguna continue, the narrower family-centered culture begins to give way to class-oriented culture.

The demand for "respect," the insistence on authority, the double standard of sexual morality and monetary responsibility, all militate against expressions of affection in the family. On the other hand, as Mexican social contacts become increasingly "secondary" instead of "face-to-face," the need for dependable friendships arises. Several

of the informal groups which have ruled the country have been based on friendships forged during the civil war, during student strikes at the universities or normal schools, or during exile for political activities. Once formed, such friendships often take precedence over any idea of the public interest, as pointed out by several outstanding Mexican students.

Shared respect is somewhat more nearly universal in Mexico. Lasswell defines it as "absence of discrimination on grounds other than merit." However, the opportunities to achieve prestige, power, and wealth are so limited in Mexico that competition may become fierce and bitter. The idea of civil service is officially accepted but of no importance in practice: "to the winner go the spoils" as in Jackson's day. Thus merit for the greatest single source of employment is usually meaningless.

Rectitude — This goal-value includes not only the dichotomous concept good-bad, but the far more fundamental idea that "each person ought to feel, think and act responsibly for the purpose of perfecting the good society (defined as the maximum sharing of all values)." This is a large and serious requirement, but obviously one crucial to a successful democracy.

It has been already reported that numerous actors in the Laguna experiment have fallen short of their goal: business men, government officials, labor representatives, *ejidatarios,* lawyers; the highly-placed and the lowly. One is tempted to compare those who complain about graft and corruption with those who wanted simply to replace old men with new (themselves) in the "Diazpotism." Nevertheless, old institutions were destroyed and new ones were created. Social change can start only with an awareness of the need for change. It can come about only when large numbers of persons share the awareness, desire a change, and reach some consensus about the direction of change. We have seen that it is only when this consensus is organized that it begins to bring results.

The realization is growing in Mexico that

the same thing can be said about wide-spread graft that Tawney said about capitalism:

The poor do not always realize that capitalism is maintained, not only by capitalists, but by those who, like many of themselves, would be capitalists if they could, and that the injustices survive, not so much because the rich exploit the poor, as because the poor, in their hearts, admire the rich.

One may now frequently read or hear such denunciations as the following by an outstanding economist, professor at the National University and former government official, Jesús Silva Hérzog:

Politics alters and corrupts everything. . . . There are big, medium and small politicians, giants and dwarfs, and they are found everywhere: in the offices and reception rooms of officials, in the schools, in the labor unions, in the co-operative societies, in the ejidos. The politician is not often considerate and honest, he is only interested in personal gain, and is a profiteer of the Revolution: in the ejido he exploits the *ejidatarios*, in the labor unions he exploits the workers and employees, and in the schools he deceives his companions. It is the easiest and most lucrative profession in Mexico. Culture is not necessary, it is a detriment; what is necessary is boldness, lack of scruples and being an authentic representative of Mexican *machismo* ("masculinity"). Everything has been corrupted. In the ejido it is common

for the peasant, exploited by the political leaders, to try in turn to exploit those who are economically weaker than he is; there are many peons working the lands of the new miniature landlord, the *ejidatario*. There has been a lack in the ejidos, as well as in the labor movement, of political education and of good teaching not only regarding rights but also regarding social duties. In the labor organizations the immorality of a good number of leaders is notorious.

A powerful challenge to the old habits was issued by the newly inaugurated president, Adolfo Ruiz Cortines, in the fall of 1952. He "cleaned house" in a number of government departments, held up the payment of bills left by his predecessor, refused to accept expensive gifts, began arriving for work at 8 a.m., obeyed traffic regulations, commended a traffic policeman for stopping his chauffeur for a forbidden U-turn, and in many other ways set a high standard of probity and responsibility for his appointees to meet. Collection of taxes was reorganized to put an end to tax evasion which, in the words of *The Financial Times of London*, "had risen to the level of an economic system." The old idea of a "law of financial responsibility" was revived; government officials elected and appointed now must declare their personal wealth and income as they take office and as they leave, with records being open to the public.

IV. ECONOMIC NATIONALISM: OIL EXPROPRIATION

The Illegality of the Expropriations

ROSCOE B. GAITHER

Roscoe B. Gaither, a New York lawyer who had been a frequent visitor to Mexico prior to 1938, was concerned over the deep animosities developing out of the oil expropriation; he was also disturbed by the "propaganda" emanating from Mexico relative to the "legality of the oil seizure." The following selection is extracted from his book, *Expropriation in Mexico: The Facts and the Law.* In the preface, he sets the tone of his work: "The Mexican people are not responsible for the chaotic situation now fermenting in Mexico. They have been deprived under the revolutionary regimes of necessary moral education previously given by the Church and for which there has been no substitute. If they accept a wrongdoing by the government of Mexico, it has been the fault of the system and not of themselves."

THE production of oil has been for a quarter of a century one of the principal industries of Mexico. In March, 1938, President Cárdenas seized practically all the property of the companies engaged in the industry. In December, 1939, the Supreme Court of Mexico declared this seizure to be a lawful expropriation. The purpose of this volume is to analyze the constitutional provisions and laws of Mexico relating to expropriation, as these have been interpreted and enforced in many decisions of the Supreme Court of Mexico over a period of many years and down to the immediate present, and to discuss from the point of view of Mexican law the seizure and the decision upholding it. First, however, the seizure of the oil properties must be seen against its political and economic background and in the light of events which preceded it. To review these antecedent events and their cul-mination is the purpose of this chapter. . . .

In 1925 the Petroleum Law was enacted, inviting foreign capital to invest in the development of oil by offering to grant new concessions and by recognizing the right to confirmation or revalidation of rights acquired before the 1917 Constitution took effect.

Oil rights in Mexico under the Petroleum Law are, therefore, of two principal kinds: rights originally acquired before May 1, 1917, and validated or recognized as valid in confirmatory, or preconstitutional, concessions issued by the Mexican Government, and rights granted in the first instance by the issuance of ordinary, or postconstitutional, concessions.

The owners of confirmatory concessions have the right in perpetuity to drill for and capture and utilize the oil which may be discovered in the subsoil of the property covered by the concession. Ordinary, or postconstitutional, concessions give the same right, but only for a limited time, which may not exceed thirty years and which is usually fixed at that period. Ordinary concessions may be cancelled only for specified defaults on the part of the owner. Confirmatory concessions are not subject to cancellation by the Government. . . .

It was on the basis of encouragement of this kind that American and British investors again risked their capital in Mexico. Suggestions and encouragements by the American Government coupled with invitations from the Mexican Government to invest, revived the decadent oil industry and production of oil began to increase until Mexico was well on the road again to be an important oil producing country. . . .

The employment of Mexican labor took on a new impetus, until in 1937 approximately eighteen thousand Mexican workmen were usually employed at higher wages than the normal rate paid for similar work in other industries, as, for example, in the railroads under government control, and always at higher wages than were paid for similar work by Petromex, the government-controlled oil company.

When the attempt to confiscate the oil industry under the terms of Article 27 of the 1917 Constitution was unsuccessful, matters in Mexico continued somewhat stable and gradually the companies began to feel that the fear of confiscation was perhaps unwarranted.

Geological and seismograph work was intensified and the Compañía Mexicana de Petróleo, El Aguila, S.A., with British capital, discovered, after an expenditure of millions of dollars in exploratory work, the oil field known as Poza Rica, in the state of Veracruz. This discovery was made before President Cárdenas took office in 1934.

From the beginning of the administration of General Cárdenas the difficulties of the oil companies increased daily. Constant threats of administrative cancellation of concessions were made, admittedly with no legal reason or basis. Drilling permits legally required to be issued were refused. Confirmatory concessions, pending since 1925 or before, were denied or unwarrantedly delayed. Transfers permitted and required under the Petroleum Regulation were tabled. The program of development suffered corresponding setbacks. . . .

Labor demands increased until on November 3, 1936, the Oil Workers' Syndicate made demands which were so far-reaching and extravagant that obviously no company could accept them and continue to exist. Discussion followed for months, but as time progressed it was evident that labor did not intend the demands to be met. Evidently preparation for some major coup was under way.

On the same day that these demands were presented to the oil companies, November 3, 1936, the Senate of the Mexican Congress approved the Expropriation Law, under authority of which President Cárdenas later seized the oil properties. This law was signed by the President on November 23 and published on November 25 in the *Diario Oficial* of Mexico. As we shall see later, the Constitution of Mexico declares that expropriation may be made only for reasons of public utility and by means of indemnity, the latter requirement meaning, the Supreme Court has repeatedly held, that payment must be made at the time of expropriation. The Law of November 23rd authorized expropriation of property for any and every reason that the ingenuity of the framers of the law could conceive, public utility being defined in the law in terms which made it include literally anything. As to indemnity, the law provided that payment might be made in a period not to exceed ten years after the expropriation.

After months of patient discussion by the companies with the Petroleum Labor Union it was quite apparent that the demands of labor were not subject to any material modification. . . .

[Here follows a list of the demands.]

All demands possible of acceptance were

conceded by the companies. A general collective contract, applicable to all the companies jointly, was demanded. The terms of this contract would have rendered further operations in Mexico impossible. The utterly unreasonable demands, obviously impossible for the companies to meet, were apparently presented with no thought in mind that there might be a compromise. That the whole purpose was to create a crisis is further shown by the result. A general strike was called which began May 28, 1937, and lasted ten days. . . .

Mexico has adopted a labor law which is very comprehensive. This law provides for labor suits to determine matters of increase or diminution of personnel and to fix hours and wages. The Labor Board established under this law, after hearing the parties in economic matters of this kind, is directed by the law to appoint a committee of three experts, who are to be advised by two commissions, one of workers and the other of employers, and who have broad powers to make "a complete study of the conflict in question, its causes and circumstances." After receiving reports of the experts, and affording full opportunity to the parties to present evidence and arguments, the Board is authorized to render its judgments. Broad powers are vested in the Board to enforce its decisions, several alternative modes of enforcement being authorized by the law.

The day after the lifting of the strike the Syndicate instituted a suit of an economic nature before the Board for the purpose of determining the economic capacity of the oil companies and their ability to pay the increased wages demanded. The provisions for a suit for this purpose, which are intended for the protection of employers, do not include questions of management or control.

The economic suit was tried before a board composed of three members who were representatives, respectively, of labor, capital, and the Government. The government representative is always supposed to be neutral, but in view of the statements of President Cárdenas which have been quoted, there could have been little doubt as to how he would vote. However, as though to eliminate any doubt whatever as to the outcome, President Cárdenas appointed a special representative to sit as a member of the Board for the sole purpose of trying the oil case. Making this appointment in a manner distinct from that provided in the law, he selected the member whose vote would be controlling and thus, in effect, created the tribunal.

Over a period of many years, the books of the oil companies had been inspected annually, and often at more frequent intervals, by government tax inspectors. They had never found any serious fault with the general accounting system used by the companies. But the committee of experts, appointed by the Labor Board to ascertain the capacity of the companies to pay, now claimed that this accounting system, which was the same as that used by oil companies throughout the world, was inefficient! Asserting that many items entered as losses should have been entered as profits, the committee had no difficulty in arriving at the conclusion that the companies were able to pay what was demanded. The committee's highly technical report, containing some fifteen hundred pages and involving a complete study of the entire accounting of all of the companies for several years, was made by the government experts in the record time of thirty days.

On the basis of the report of this committee, the Labor Board, on December 18, 1937, rendered a decision against the companies in the economic suit. Ten days later the companies took an appeal. On March 1, 1938, the Supreme Court of Mexico rendered a decision upholding in all respects the decision of the Labor Board and denying any rights to the companies in the economic suit. . . .

The companies, within the time allowed them by law, offered to pay the increase of twenty-six million pesos demanded by labor, and to conform with the decision in every way except only as to the surrender of management. This offer to meet the economic demands was not accepted, because, according to President Cárdenas, it was made "too late." Six days later he seized all the property of the companies. But during that interval of six days the Syndicate and the Labor Board went through the form of further proceedings.

One of the methods provided by the Labor Law for enforcing a decision of the Labor Board, or penalizing a failure to comply with a decision, is to declare the labor contract cancelled to hold the employer liable for a sum based on the salaries of the workers, the duration of their employment, and the period of the contract, plus damages for losses resulting from the conflict. This was the method elected by the Syndicate.

On March 17, 1938, seventeen days after the decision of the Labor Board which was declared to be a contract, the companies' offer to pay the twenty-six million peso increase in wages having meanwhile been made and rejected, the Syndicate petitioned the Board to declare the contract, or quasi-contract, broken by the companies and to order the companies to pay three months' salaries, plus damages, in conformity with the provisions of the law applicable in the case of such a breach as was alleged.

The next day, March 18, 1938, at eleven o'clock in the morning, the Labor Board had prepared a decision denying the petition of the Syndicate. But at two o'clock in the afternoon of the same day, the Board rendered a different decision, declaring the contract which it had created cancelled and ordering the companies to pay their employees three months' salaries plus additional damages, the amount of which was to be later determined.

The immediate practical result of this decision, whatever its legal validity might be, was that the companies had no labor contracts and no employees who were members of the Petroleum Union and that they were liable to their former employees for large sums of money, the amount of which was in part fixed and in part still to be determined.

On March 18, President Cárdenas signed his Expropriation Decree. It was published in the Diario Oficial of that same date, which actually appeared on the 19th. On the same day property of all kinds belonging to the oil companies in various parts of Mexico was forcibly seized.

The reason given for the expropriation was fear of a crisis arising from the cancellation of the labor contract. The companies, whose property was seized, had, of course, no more to do with the cancellation than they had to do with the making of the supposed contract. . . .

From a narrative of the events preceding the seizure of the oil properties, it is evident that whatever crisis may have existed on March 18, 1938, or appeared to be impending, was wholly the result of successive steps which were designed to precipitate a crisis and thus to give some semblance of an occasion for the seizure.

That the strike and the economic suit did not have higher wages and more favorable working conditions for their real purpose is obvious. If commentary were needed to expose the design underlying the successive steps which were taken jointly by the labor organization and the Government, it may be found in the statements which have been quoted from President Cárdenas and from the platform setting forth the Six-Year Plan.

Further evidence of such intent is afforded by a statement made by Lombardo Toledano, the head of the Mexican Confederation of Workers, to a correspondent of The New York Times with regard to the offer by the companies to pay the increase of twenty-six million pesos a year. He said: "This offer Cárdenas refused. If we had accepted, it would have been a victory of labor over capital; but by refusing the offer, it was a great victory of the Mexican people against foreign imperialism."

President Cárdenas said the offer was made "too late" because the purpose from the outset had been to seize the properties and the opportunity so carefully created could not now be passed over.

The Expropriations Were Legal and Necessary

MEXICAN GOVERNMENT

In 1940 the question of payment for the expropriated properties was still far from settled and, therefore, a cause of dissension between the two governments at a time (immediately after the outbreak of the European war) when cooperation was essential. The Mexican government made its appeal to the United States public through a carefully reasoned and somewhat legalistic approach. The publication was in the form of a reply to two publications from the Standard Oil Company.

THE oil situation, both national and international, had been definitely settled, legally and politically. Legally, with the enactment of the law of December 26, 1925, together with its regulatory provisions; politically, with the satisfactory termination of the international controversy which had been raised by the oil companies and ended with the full recognition and acceptance of the legal petroleum provisions and the regulations thereunder, on the one side, and on the other, by the acquiescence in the principle that in the future, any question arising relative thereto, would be disposed of in accordance with said laws before the Mexican Courts and Administrative Departments.

In view of the foregoing, the Government of President Cárdenas limited its action to the legal and international situations already established. The oil companies continued the oil exploitation subject to the Regulatory Measures, under which they could continue enjoying the powers granted for the exploration and exploitation of oil and utilizing that which they could find in the subsoil of the oil lands covered by the confirmatory and ordinary concessions that the Mexican Nation had granted to them in accordance with the existing laws.

The Standard Oil Company of New Jersey and the other foreign companies that exploited the oil in Mexico, deliberately sought to create the impression, both within and outside the country, that the policy of President Cárdenas' Administration was to bring to a head the final realization of a plan conceived by the various governments of Mexico, since the administration of President Carranza, the effect of which was to dispossess the foreign interests, which were controlling the petroleum industry, of their alleged property rights, by nationalizing their properties.

Such an assertion is palpably false, since the action taken by the Government of President Cárdenas was not, properly speaking, a continuation of the constitutional and political actions which had been developed by previous Administrations, but had a distinct and independent character of its own, made necessary by reason of subsequent developments. . . .

The Government of President Cárdenas did not issue any new oil laws regulating Article 27 of the Constitution, but merely followed the legal status already existing. It was only when it found itself compelled, by the rebellious and defiant conduct of the oil companies, that it decreed the expropriation of their properties, including, of course, the concessions which the Mexican Nation had granted to them for the exploration and exploitation of oil, as aforesaid. It has already been seen that the laws mentioned

From *The True Facts About the Expropriation of the Oil Companies' Properties in Mexico* (Mexico, 1940), pp. 69–91.

had been expressly recognized by the Government of the United States as constituting what it deemed sufficient as a final settlement of the international controversies that had arisen prior to the advent of the present Administration. . . .

The petroleum workers requested of the various companies that operated in Mexico, the revision of their labor contracts. This was a voluntary act on the part of the unions which merely exercised a right that is fully recognized in all the civilized countries. As the unions and the companies were not able to reach an agreement regarding the terms of the new contract, the workers decided to call a strike, which is also a lawful right universally recognized by all, except those countries which function under a totalitarian system of government.

The strike continued for some time without the parties being able to reach an agreement, and, as the shortage of fuel caused by the strike was threatening the very existence of Mexico's economic life, the Government deemed itself compelled, for the first time, to intervene in the conflict. After endeavoring, unsuccessfully, to find a solution, the Government recommended that the workers return to their work and to submit their case to the Federal Labor Board at Mexico City.

Said Labor Board, after considering the opinions of three governmental experts who had carefully studied the various phases of the controversy, and after hearing the expert testimony of the consultants appointed by both the oil companies and the workers, rendered its award, placing itself on a fair level between what the workers' union demanded and what the companies were willing to concede.

Just as soon as the decision of the Federal Labor Board was publicly announced, the companies emphatically stated through the press in Mexico, and in the United States, that they were not disposed to submit to the decision of the Authorities, and that if the Supreme Court of Mexico, to which an appeal had already been taken, did not

grant the application for review of the award rendered by the Federal Labor Board, they would abandon the operation of their properties. In thus assuming such an attitude, they were merely observing their accustomed rebellious conduct towards the legally constituted Mexican Authorities. . . .

The Supreme Court, after a careful study, held that the decision of the Board did not contain any constitutional violations and that, therefore, said award could not be reversed.

Both before and after the Court rendered its decision, several efforts for conciliation were made by various high officials, and even by the President himself, offering fair and concrete suggestions to both parties with a view to putting an end to the dispute. Inasmuch as the companies maintained that the decision required an expenditure of more than twenty-six million pesos, the Mexican Government offered to appoint a commission that would supervise, under the guarantee of the Federal Executive, the enforcement of the Board's decision, in order to guarantee to the companies that they would not pay more than the aforesaid amount. The Government also suggested that in order to clarify the meaning of some of the provisions of the award, the parties agree to a binding interpretation of those provisions which the companies feared might deprive them of the necessary freedom to manage their business economically and efficiently.

At a meeting held in the President's office, the companies' representatives definitely stated that they would not accept the Government's suggestions.

When notice of the Federal Labor Board's award of December 18, 1937, was served on the foreign companies, requiring them to put into operation the new working conditions, they once more refused to abide by said award which, as already seen, had been held constitutional by the Supreme Court of Mexico. . . .

Realizing that the rebellious attitude of the oil companies would bring about, inevitably, a total suspension of activities throughout the petroleum industry, President Cárdenas, in the exercise of the powers granted to the Federal Executive by paragraph 2, of Article 27 of the Constitution, as well as by the Law of Expropriation, on March 18, 1938, decreed the expropriation for cause of public utility, of the real and personal properties belonging to the oil companies who had refused to abide by the Federal Labor Board's award, as aforesaid.

Under these circumstances, what alternative was there left to the Government? Could it permit noncompliance with a decision rendered by a legitimate authority and confirmed by the Highest Tribunal of the Country? Can anyone imagine that any foreign corporation in any other country would be permitted to look with contempt upon and refuse to obey the decision of the Highest Court of the land? Could the Mexican Government permit the companies to carry out their threat that they would close down their plants and stop the entire production of the fuel used all over Mexico?

This situation was discussed in detail by President Cárdenas in a speech which he made to the Mexican Nation, on March 18, 1938, using the following language:

Production of fuel is essential for the many activities of the country, and especially for transportation. A stoppage or insufficiency of production or even production at prohibitive cost due to difficulties which would have to be surmounted, would soon cause a crisis which would threaten not only our progress, but even the very peace of the country. Many of the principal phases of banking and commerce would be paralyzed. Public works of general interest would become next to impossible. The existence of the Government itself would be seriously imperiled. If the State once lost its economic power, its political power would be lost and chaos would result.

It is self evident that the refusal of the oil companies to comply with the decision of the highest Judicial Court creates a problem for the Executive Power not of the mere enforcement of a judgment, but a decisive problem which calls for an urgent solution. Such a solution is imperative for the social interest of all of the laboring classes in all industries of the country. All Mexicans and even foreigners residing here have a public interest in this solution; they need not alone the power of fuel, but peace. It is the very sovereignty of the Nation which would continually be exposed to simple manipulations of foreign capital, which forgetful of the fact that it has been organized in the form of Mexican corporations under Mexican law, nevertheless is attempting to evade mandates and obligations when compliance has been ordered by the Authorities of the country.

The case is clear and evident. The Government is compelled to apply the Law of Expropriation now in force, not only to exact obedience and respect from the oil companies, but by reason of the fact that the award of the labor authorities terminated the labor contracts between the companies and their workmen. Unless the Government took possession of the companies' plants, immediate paralysis of the petroleum industry would ensue, and all other industries and the general economy of the country would suffer incalculable damage.

It is alleged . . . that the confiscatory procedure followed by the Mexican Government was accelerated greatly, beginning with the year 1930; it is alleged . . . as an undisputed fact, that on that date the Mexican Government enacted a Labor Code of general application, in order to foster collective bargaining between workers and employers, and to establish courts for the settlement of disputes between them. The true fact is that it was designed solely and fundamentally, because of the necessity of establishing rules, forms and conditions, regulatory in their nature, between workers and employers by means of a system based on numerous existing Mexican precedents. It is a known fact that, by the time said Code was enacted, there were several concerns in the country operating on a collective bargaining basis, and that there were in existence already, several Labor Courts.

It is difficult to conceive how the Standard Oil Company can assert that the Mexican Government had a premeditated intention of confiscating the oil companies' properties, merely because the Government selected the same route followed by other civilized countries, inasmuch as it is known that labor laws, courts and collective bargaining contracts exist everywhere. Certainly, it is unreasonable to classify the evolution of that character of legislation as a general or world-wide tendency towards confiscation.

The explanation of this absurd interpretation made by the Standard Oil Company must be sought in the fact that all intervention by the Government in this field of activity, necessarily resulted in placing limitations and restrictions on the abusive practices employed by the companies regarding the treatment of their workers, both economically and socially. It came within the realm of possibility in a great many instances, to restrain those abuses, due precisely to the enactment of those laws that compelled the companies, much to their dislike, to take into consideration the human needs and sufferings of their workers. . . .

The Federal Executive in decreeing the expropriation, based his action upon the following constitutional provisions:

1. Article 27 of the Constitution, second paragraph, of subparagraph VI, provides:

The Federal and State laws shall determine within their respective jurisdictions those cases in which the taking of private property shall be considered of public utility: and in accordance with the said laws the administrative authorities shall make the corresponding declaration. The amount fixed as compensation for the expropriated *thing* shall be based on the sum of which the said property shall be valued for fiscal purposes in the cadastral or revenue offices, whether this value be that manifested by the owner or merely impliedly accepted by reason of the payment of his taxes on such a basis. The increased value which the property in question may have acquired through improvements made subsequent to the date of the fixing of the fiscal value shall be the only matter subject to expert appraisal and to judicial determination. The same procedure shall be observed in respect to objects whose value is not recorded in the revenue offices.

2. Article I, paragraphs V, VII, X, . . . [and Articles] VIII and XX, of the Expropriation Law of November 23, 1936, respectively, contain the following provisions:

Article I. — It shall be deemed as a public use: . . . V. — The satisfaction of collective needs in case of war or internal disturbances; the supply to cities and centers of population with foodstuffs or other articles of necessary use, and all means employed to combat or prevent the propagation of epidemics, fires, plagues, floods, or other public calamities; . . . VII. — The defense, preservation, development or use of the natural resources susceptible of exploitation; . . . X. — The necessary measures to prevent the destruction of the natural resources and whatever damages might be suffered by property in detriment to society.

Articles VIII. — In such cases as paragraph V, VII and X, of Article I herein referred to, the Federal Executive, after proclamation, may order the seizure of such properties as are subject to expropriation or temporary occupation, or decree the immediate execution of provisions concerning limitation as to ownership; provided, that the filing of the administrative remedy for revocation thereof shall not suspend the seizure of the particular property or properties, or the execution of provisions concerning limitation of ownership. . . .

Article XX. — The authorities decreeing the condemnation shall fix the manner and periods of time in which compensation shall be paid, which periods shall never be longer than ten years.

Relying on these constitutional and statutory provisions, the Executive of the Union, on March 18, 1938, issued his Decree of Expropriation, for cause of public utility of the movable and immovable properties of the oil companies as may be necessary, in the opinion of the Department of National Economy, for the discovery, extraction, storage, refinery and distribution of the products of the petroleum industry.

They provided further that the Department of National Economy, and the Department of the Treasury intervening therein as administrator of the properties of the nation, shall proceed to the immediate occupation of the properties which were the subject of the expropriation and to draw the respective deed of seizure. . . .

It is a well-known principle of Constitutional Law, which has been affirmed repeatedly by the Supreme Court of the United States, that all private properties acquired from a government, including those held under grant, or contract, are subject to the right of eminent domain. A charter or contract, as the case may be, from the States, is not a title legally superior to a title to land, and it can, therefore, condemn it by paying a fair compensation, in which case the taking over of such rights or powers granted by the State does not impair the right of property. (Green v. Riddle, 8 Wall. 5; Milner v. New Jersey R. Tramp Co., 3 Wall. 782; 18 Law. ed., 799; Richmond J.P.R. Co., v. Dix, 6 How. 507; 12 Law. ed. 535; New Orleans, Gas Light and Heat Producing and Mfg. Co., 115 U.S. 650; 29 Law. ed., 516.)

It must be concluded, as will hereafter be seen, that the only compensation which the State is obligated to pay when it expropriates a concession, is the equivalent of the amount which was actually paid to the State or a political subdivision thereof as consideration for the grant. This principle has been repeatedly recognized by the laws and the jurisprudence of the United States.

Concessions of franchise generally, and more particularly franchises to conduct the business of a private concern, although protected by the constitutional guarantee which gives them the right to contract freely and to acquire, possess and dispose of property — "are not donations to a utility of property by the use of which profit may be made. They are privileges granted to utilities to enable them to employ their property in the public service and make a profit out of such use of that property. As stated in the New Hampshire statute, 'all such franchises, rights and privileges being granted in the public interest only' are not justly subject to capitalization against the public" — as was categorically declared by Justice Brandeis in United Railway v. West, 280 U.S., 234, at 257, in which he reviews the decisions of the Supreme Court of the United States.

The legality of the Expropriation Decree for cause of public utility, by the payment of fair compensation, issued by the Government of President Cárdenas, expropriating movable and immovable properties of the oil companies, is evident and therefore, said properties have not been "confiscated" as is falsely asserted in the pamphlet published by the Standard Oil Company, but, on the contrary, said properties have legally become a part of the Nation's patrimony by virtue of the proper exercise of a national and international sovereign act.

The Standard Oil Company expressly admits that the Mexican Government, acting through its various governmental agencies, has, on several occasions, made known its intention to pay a fair compensation for the properties expropriated. It states that President Cárdenas, his Secretary of Foreign Affairs, and the Mexican Ambassador at Washington, have reiterated Mexico's willingness to pay the oil companies, but that the latter have consistently and systematically refused to consider the matter of payment.

The Mexican Government has made diligent efforts to do whatever is necessary, not only to effect an appraisal of the expropriated properties but also to fix the method of payment; using as a basis to arrive at a fair valuation, that which will truly represent the real interests involved in this controversy. As a matter of fact the question of appraisal of property values would have been terminated long ago, had the oil companies been willing to cooperate, through direct negotiations with the Mexican Government. Said companies, however, have refused to discuss the question of valuation and, likewise, refused to appear before the courts, as is required by law in such cases.

The obvious inference is, therefore, that the obstinacy of the companies in thus opposing friendly negotiations and refusing to comply with the proceedings established by law, is due to the belief which they entertain that the appraisal of their properties will never reach that imaginary and fantastic figure they have maliciously permitted to run rampant in the public mind.[1]

In view of the foregoing, and to offset the unfounded propaganda mentioned, the Mexican Officials, as a result of special studies, corroborated by ample documentary evidence, have found both in law and in reason, the basis on which to make the appraisals, some of which are the following:

I. That provided by subparagraph two, paragraph VI, of Article 27 of the Mexican Constitution, which provides that real property, and not the equipment, should be appraised at its tax valuation.

I. The other properties belonging to the companies must be appraised by experts, who shall apply those general rules, on appraisal of properties that are customarily used.

III. The payment to the companies for the concessions shall be made in accordance with the amount of the expenses incurred in obtaining them from the State, following, in this instance, the practice prevailing also in the United States, as will be shown hereinafter.

IV. Unpaid taxes recognized as due and

[1] Nearly $500,000,000. [Editor's note.]

owing by the companies, and which may be pending before the Tax Courts of Mexico before the date when the expropriation was decreed, shall be deducted, as well as such amounts as the workers are entitled to collect.

With regard to the last matter mentioned in the foregoing paragraph, the companies admit that they would be obligated to pay to the workmen the three months' salary claimed by them, in the event that they had been left without employment. However, since the Government employed them immediately, no time was lost by them.

Even assuming that their contention is correct (although it is not so, because if an employer breaches his contract he is liable to pay the corresponding compensation whether or not the employee finds work elsewhere) it must be borne in mind that the companies had voluntarily bound themselves by a collective contract with the workers. Said contract provided for the payment of pensions and a certain amount of cash to the workers on the termination of the contract which was based upon length of service; under those conditions, either the new Administration had to assume the obligations of the oil companies in favor of the workers as of the date when they entered the service of the petroleum industry, in which case the Government is entitled to receive the amounts held in trust by them for such purposes, or the Government assumes the obligations to pay them as of the date of the new contract, in which latter case, the workers are entitled to receive compensation from the companies for their seniority rights under their old contracts.

A Historic, Irrepressible Conflict

HARLOW S. PERSON

Shortly before the final settlement of the dispute between the oil companies and the Mexican government, "an executive who desired a brief statement of the Mexican oil problem" requested Harlow S. Person to draft a memorandum on the subject. Person, a New York consultant in Business Economics and Management, complied and then, at the behest of some of those who read the memorandum, published his essay as a small book in 1942.

ONE who is privileged to examine the quarter-century of oil controversy in detail derives therefrom the impression that actual expropriation was probably not the primary objective of the most responsible Mexican leaders. Control through effective regulation apparently was their objective. Of course expropriation was never absent from the minds of the local politicians. It was something definite that the uneducated mass could comprehend, and the leaders in their political campaigning worked the idea for all it was worth. Perhaps in so doing they generated a force which in the end could not be resisted.

Most of the official acts up to the moment of expropriation had the character of steps toward strong regulatory control of the industry. The passage in 1936 of an act authorizing expropriation was regarded as a convenient, powerful tool for use in negotiations with the companies. There is testimony of officials close to President Cárdenas on the fateful day of expropriation — March 18, 1938 — that to the last moment he preferred regulation and yielded to expropriation only under the impelling pressure of events. These pressures were those of public opinion, of the less responsible local leaders, of the Petroleum Workers' Union and, perhaps the most decisive, an obstinate resistance of the oil companies

that in the minds of the Mexicans raised the questions as to where the sovereignty of Mexico was lodged. It should be noted that not all foreign-held and operated properties were expropriated — the Gulf Oil Company properties, for instance. The expropriation decree affected only the companies that felt strong enough to offer vigorous resistance to the government and declare they would not be responsible for the ultimate consequences of adverse court and administrative decisions. . . .

The Constitution of 1917 . . . restated fundamental Mexican law and declared that the legal ownership of petroleum and hydrocarbons — solid, liquid or gaseous — is vested in the nation; that only Mexicans and Mexican companies have the right to acquire ownership of resources or obtain concessions to develop them, although foreigners could acquire such concessions under limited conditions; that private property shall not be expropriated except for reasons of public welfare; that there shall be indemnification for expropriated property; and that the amount of indemnification shall be based on the sum at which the property is valued for purposes of taxation plus 10 per cent. (The 10 per cent addition was later eliminated by amendment.)

Concerning this constitution several observations are pertinent. By those identified with leftist views throughout the world it was hailed as the most advanced of national charters; by conservatives it was deplored as a symbol of a dangerous world trend. Any objective analysis must conclude that it reflected the deep-seated feelings of the Mexican people, and that Mexican military-political leaders were influenced by the implicit social philosophy for the very reason that this philosophy reflected such feelings. These leaders sought followers — for armies when the military technique was employed, and for votes when the technique followed constitutional lines — and to secure followers they wasted no time with doctrines to which the mass of Mexican citizens was not already sensitive. The Mexican people wanted a standard of living higher than mere subsistence; they wanted a better condition than that of peonage; and they believed that the better condition would never be achieved so long as agricultural lands were held by a relatively small number of owners and foreign corporations were draining the surplus of income from the rich oil and other natural resources out of the country. They believed the Díaz regime had sold them down the river, and they were willing to follow the leader who promised most toward correcting the conditions.

Although the substance of the constitution may have expressed the will of a sovereign people, it created consternation among several strong group interests. Two of these were domestic and for them adjustment was a domestic problem. To the proprietors of haciendas it threatened a ruin similar to that which had come to the landed gentry of the southern states of the United States during the War Between the States — although it proved not to be so drastic. To the Catholic Church, still a substantial landholder, it threatened some impairment of its revenues and especially of its hold on the people through a clergy that was then largely Spanish. The third group was not domestic, and adjustment involved a conflict in foreign relations, for to foreign investors it threatened destruction of the privileges acquired during the

Díaz regime. In their eyes it meant "confiscation" of properties (which they had expected to yield abundant returns through many years), higher taxes, higher costs of operation, less of an opportunity to claim and capitalize the future. These were powerful groups, and their opposition to making the provisions of the constitution effective was immediate and both open and undercover. Consequently the decade of Carranza and his immediate successors was not one of smooth implementation of the constitution. It was a period of conflicts with the special interest groups, now primarily with one, now primarily with another. It was a period also during which administrations had to face an opposition of people who were restless with the slow progress toward the better conditions which they imagined could be established promptly. . . .

[By 1934] industrial labor felt an especial bitterness concerning the dominating control of Mexican resources by foreign companies, and as their unions acquired strength they were able to exercise an increasingly strong influence on government.

With respect to such influence the Petroleum Workers' Union was in an especially favorable position. It was the union of workers in an industry closely identified with despised foreign interests. And although working conditions in this industry did not compare unfavorably with those elsewhere in Mexico, they were not such as the workers believed the economy of the industry could stand. Also the workers held as a grievance the fact that although there had been marked increase in technical skill among them, advancement went generally to foreigners. They were ripe for exertion of their influence.

A strike of the workers of oil company "El Aguila" in 1934, aimed immediately at equalization of wages, led to arbitration by President Rodríguez himself, and eventually to the setting up of regional commissions to consider grievances and make awards. Each commission consisted of three members — a federal labor inspector, a representative of the interested labor organization and a representative of the company concerned. During 1934, 1935 and 1936 there were a number of demands, strikes, hearings and awards, the details of which are now unimportant. The significant things are: first, a broadening of the scope of the workers' demands, integration and consolidation of the various local petroleum workers' organizations, strengthening of the Petroleum Workers' Union and unification of its demands to apply to all companies; and second, an absence of sympathy with labor's objectives on the part of the companies and a strengthening thereby of their unified resistance.

The pressures of the unions increased. Eventually, on November 3, 1936, the companies received a voluminous document of demands from the Petroleum Workers' Union. This document of 175 mimeographed foolscap pages had been in process of preparation by the First Grand Extraordinary Convention of the Union during a period of nearly a year. The scope of the matters on which the workers demanded a collective agreement is indicated by the following chapter headings: 1. General Provisions; 2. Employment, Vacancies, Promotions, and Personnel Changes in General; 3. Reduction of Personnel, Resignations, and Respective Compensation; 4; Dismissal, Discipline, and Expulsion; 5. General Working Conditions; 6. Work Shifts, Hours, Wages, and Overtime; 7. Transfers and Mobilizations; 8. Sickness and Medical Attention in General; 9. Compensation, Safety, and Hygiene; 10. Pensions; 11. Rest Days, Vacations, and Leaves; 12. Savings Funds; 13. Scholarships; 14. Trade Apprentices; 15. Mexican and Foreign Technicians; 16. Departmental Delegates; 17. Check-off of Union Dues; 18. Housing; 19. Libraries, Schools, Promotion of Sports, and Recreation Grounds; 20. Passes and Means of Transportation; 21. Promotion List and Seniority; 22. Tools and Implements; 23 Miscellaneous Provisions; 24. Wage Scale and Classification of Categories.

There is nothing in this document, one of the last mile-stones on the route that led in time to expropriation, that suggests colonial or quasi-colonial labor mentality. It is an impressive, far-reaching schedule of items for inclusion in labor contracts. Some were imitative of the best in other countries; some more advanced but worthy of consideration; a few almost fantastic, such as free transportation for families of workers on vacation with full pay.

On the refusal of the companies to agree to the demands, a strike was threatened for the nineteenth of November. Because a strike would be extremely serious for the industry and prejudicial to the national interest, President Cárdenas through the Department of Labor succeeded in having it deferred and in securing an agreement for a worker-employer assembly for consideration of the entire problem. The conferences of this assembly lasted for nearly six months of proposals, counterproposals, conditional counterproposals, and intermittent wrangling. In May, 1937, at the end of a short recess the companies submitted certain points of agreement. These were unacceptable to the union, which insisted on the full range of its demands, and at the end of May the strike was put into effect and oil production was stopped. It is possible that, had the union been less insistent, the outcome of expropriation might have been deferred for a considerable period.

In the meantime the Mexican Congress had fashioned a strong weapon to strengthen the position of the government in its insistence that the demands of the workers be met in a substantial measure reflecting economic capacity, and in its efforts generally to bring the industry under regulatory control. This new weapon, an Expropriation Law confirmed on November 23, 1936, also could serve the government well in case an issue which it feared — Who Governs Mexico? — should actually become defined. In any case the availability of this law should have strong influence in the effort to establish regulation.

. . . The Constitution of 1917 carried the unusual provision already noted that, when a strike involves issues which by their special nature cannot be resolved through the ordinary type of collective bargaining, appeal to proper authorities may be made on the grounds of a "conflict of economic order." Accordingly, after about a week of strike the union, undoubtedly after consultation with the government (as would probably be the case in any nation), appealed to the Federal Board of Mediation and Arbitration on the ground that such a conflict was involved. The board accepted the appeal and, having thus lifted the controversy to a higher level, ordered the strike suspended. There were six months of hearings, special committee investigations, briefs and arguments, and finally, on December 18, 1937, the board, hastened by a new eleven-day strike of impatience, rendered its decision. On the grounds of public welfare it confirmed essentially all the union non-wage demands, and awarded the workers a wage increase which the companies calculated would aggregate 41 million pesos a year. The government calculation was a little over 26 million pesos.

The oil companies refused to accept the decision. The principal arguments of objection were that the industry was economically unable to carry the wage increase and other cost involved, and that provisions concerning approval by the union of the appointment of certain supervisors (the early question of promotion) took management out of the hands of the owners. They made newspaper appeals, including strongly implied threats of refusing to accept responsibility for consequences that might arise from the situation; in fact many full-page advertisements had the tone of appeals to the people against the government and incensed the former intensely. Finally they applied to the Mexican Supreme Court for an injunction to prevent the decision from taking effect.

While the appeal for an injunction was under consideration by the court, the companies negotiated on the side with the Cárdenas government. They suggested that they might be able to meet the wage increase provided relief were had from other items of the award, especially those concerned with the appointment of supervising employees. The government stood firm on the board's award and refused to respond to the suggestions of the companies.

The Supreme Court rendered a decision on March 1, 1938, to the effect that the decision of the Labor Board was in conformity with the constitution and the authorities should proceed to enforce terms of the award. The Labor Board gave the companies a week within which to endorse the award. The companies protested; the decision did not make them more able to meet the increased costs, they declared. They thereupon appealed to a district court for suspension of the award, which was granted temporarily but within a few days definitely refused. Then the union appeared before the Labor Board with charges that the companies were in *rebeldía* — i.e., refused to recognize constitutional, judicial and administrative procedures. On March 18, 1938, the board declared the companies were in *rebeldía* and all existing contracts were canceled.

. . . Testimony of an intimate associate of President Cárdenas at the time is to the effect that the president preferred to avoid expropriation; that in general he wanted the oil industry brought under effective regulatory control, and in particular he wanted mutually acceptable relations with labor worked out throught collective bargaining. But the sweep of events, a consequential part of which was the more effective maneuvering of the leaders of the union, the sequence of administrative and court decisions in accordance with due processes in favor of the latter, and finally the ill-advised obstinacy and irritating and challenging declaration of the companies that they would no longer be responsible for the consequences, led him to the decision on the evening of March 18, 1938, that the question of whether foreign private corporations were greater than the government was involved. He declared expropriation of the properties of those oil companies engaged in conflict with labor — all the large ones but not all the companies — by a decree of which the preamble was as follows:

Whereas it is of public knowledge that the oil companies operating in the country and which were ordered to establish new working conditions on December 18 last by Group Number Seven of the Federal Board of Conciliation and Arbitration have expressed their refusal to abide by the Award rendered, notwithstanding the recognition of its constitutionality by the Supreme Court of Justice of the Nation, without adducing reasons for said refusal other than an alleged financial incapacity, which has brought about as a necessary consequence the application of Article 123, Fraction XXI, of the General Constitution of the Republic, to the effect that the competent authority declare the labor contracts derived from the said Award to be terminated; and

Whereas this fact produces as an inevitable result the total suspension of activities in the oil industry and in these circumstances it is urgent that the Public Power take adequate steps to prevent serious internal disturbances that would make the satisfaction of collective needs and the furnishing of necessary consumption goods to all centers of population impossible in view of the resulting paralysis of the means of transportation and of the productive industries, as well as to provide for the protection, conservation, development, and exploitation of the wealth contained in the petroleum deposits and to adopt measures tending to prevent damages to the properties, to the detriment of the community, all of which circumstances being considered sufficient to decree the expropriation of the properties engaged in petroleum production; . . .

Consideration of all the details of the controversy here presented in bare outline leads to the conclusion that it was an historic, irrepressible conflict. One party to the conflict, expressing itself through an agency identified with labor, was the government of a people recently emerged from feudal status to that of a society democratic in form and organized under a constitutional charter. The irrepressible in this party's point of view was that the natural resources of the country — for centuries a public domain in common law — had, through conquistadorial processes merging into the more subtle processes of purchase from irresponsible transitory governments, become the exclusive property of limited special interests, and must therefore be restored to the *dominium directum* of the people in substance as they had been restored in form by the Constitution of 1917. It was the irrepressibility of the deep-seated emotions and the will of a sovereign people. While the procedures by which parties to the conflict pursued their ends were within the frame of constitutional sanctions, in many details they were characteristic of political maneuvering — sometimes specious, opportunistic and unrealistic. The 175 foolscap pages of the union's document of November 3, 1936, comprised demands for betterment of labor conditions generally in advance of what prevailed in the older democracies of western Europe and the United States, and in instances whimsical. If the government had not been from the beginning sympathetic with an ultimate outcome of effective regulatory control, and expropriation if it were unavoidable, it might perhaps have secured very considerable modification of these demands and the establishment of a *modus vivendi* as between the employers and the workers. But regulatory control, which instead of becoming stronger was breaking down to an alarming degree, and later unequivocal acknowledgment of national sovereignty appear to have been the principal concern of the government, rather than merely improvement of labor conditions.

The other party to the conflict was a group of great foreign corporations, the irrepressible in whose point of view was that although special privileges were being progressively weakened in the older capitalistic nations, here at least, in the quasi-colonial territory of a generally uneducated people, they could salvage a large measure of their economic independence and autonomy. To them that objective appeared to be worth the struggle; especially in view of the fact that with reason they did not have a feeling of permanence and security after any negotiated settlement, and feared the final outcome would in any case be expropriation. They were aware that the national sentiment was as much against foreign capital as against monopoly. The companies did not know how far democratic processes might go, could not foresee how soon the Mexican democracy would become stabilized not only under a substantive charter but within procedural legislation.

It is interesting to note parenthetically that the 1936 labor laws of Venezuela, to the oil fields of which country the oil companies were transferring their investments and to whose labor laws they promptly adjusted, provided for labor conditions essentially as extreme as those demanded by the Mexican workers. The exceptional factor was that the Venezuelan unions were very much more restricted and "stabilized" by national law. What the companies feared most in Mexico, apparently, were not the labor demands per se but what they considered the irresponsibility of labor organizations, their political character and power in politics, and the possibility of their forcing eventual expropriation. To the Mexican people the companies' fear was that the unions had the power to cause enforcement of the letter of the law for the first time in Mexican history.

The government of Mexico may be criticized by history for ruthlessness within constitutional forms. The companies may be criticized for having taken an attitude of being outside and above the law, and for having in large measure generated the causes of irrepressible conflict. The Mexican people were impatient of evolutionary processes; the companies were intolerant of and refused to recognize them.

V. ECONOMIC POLICY: INDUSTRIALIZATION

Industrialization Is Possible

SANFORD A. MOSK

Sanford A. Mosk, Professor of Economics at the University of California, made a thorough study of the Mexican economic situation in a book entitled *Industrial Revolution in Mexico*. Although he was confident that the nation had adequate resources for substantial industrial development, he feared that industrialization would progress at too fast a rate for the other sectors of the economy and society.

PART III of this study dealt with the problems of industrialization in Mexico, as they revolve about the size of the internal market, the supply of capital and credit, the training of labor, technicians, and management, the tendency toward inflation, and the balance of payments. These are the major problems, and they suggest the bottlenecks that are likely to be prominent in Mexico as the industrialization process goes forward.

The list of problems could, of course, be readily extended. One question which naturally arises relates to sources of raw materials for manufacturing. In specific cases, shortages will doubtless develop as industry expands. In general, however, Mexico has reasonably good sources of industrial raw materials; her principal deficiency is in agricultural resources. In contrast to most of the other countries of Latin America, Mexico has both coal and iron deposits. These resources are not of the highest quality, but they are sufficiently good, and sufficiently large in amount, to support a much larger industrial structure than that which Mexico now has. The development of coal and iron resources is getting strong encour-

agement from the Mexican government. In the chemical industry, another field which is critical for further industrial development, Mexico has also good sources of basic raw materials. Broadly speaking, the principal limitations in raw materials are found in certain cases where the source is agriculture, for example, wool hard fibers.

In fuel and power, the prospects for the long run are much better than the actual supply or the supply likely to be forthcoming in the immediate future. The best and most extensively developed coal deposits are in the north, far from all industrial centers except Monterrey. The costs of transporting coal to Mexico City, Puebla, or Guadalajara are comparatively high, and great improvements in railroad facilities are needed before coal can become an important source of industrial fuel in these places. The use of petroleum for generating industrial power, although fairly common in the Mexico City area, has been handicapped by high costs and by irregularities in supply. Ever since the oil industry was nationalized in 1938 it has been going through the throes of reorganization, and it is apparent that more time will be

From Sanford A. Mosk, *Industrial Revolution in Mexico*, University of California Press (Berkeley, 1950), pp. 304–311. Reprinted by permission of the publishers, University of California Press.

needed before the industry will be able to settle down to orderly and regular production schedules. Further additions to refining capacity are also needed, at considerable cost. It is not likely, therefore, that the supply of fuel oil for use in industry will undergo a rapid expansion.

In the past several years the Mexican government has been vigorously pursuing the development of hydroelectric power resources, with the objective of providing additional sources of industrial power as well as more residential lighting. The Federal Electricity Commission created in 1937 has been planning and constructing new projects, and it has also attempted to bring about greater coördination in the use of existing power facilities, both public and private. Substantial increases in the generation of electric power have been achieved, in spite of the difficulties of getting new equipment during and since the war. Nevertheless, the supply has not kept pace with the industrial demand, and critical shortages have occurred from time to time, with serious consequences for industrial production in the Mexico City district. The possibilities for further hydroelectric power development are great. It is estimated that only about 8 per cent of Mexico's potential hydroelectric capacity has been utilized. It must be recognized, however, that substantial developments in this field will call for huge amounts of public investment, and, in view of all the other claims upon public financial support, the government may not be able to keep up the rate of power expansion required by the growth of industry.

This last proposition actually should be stated in reverse. The development of power is a prerequisite for the development of industry, especially in the industrial district of Mexico City. In the immediate future it is more important for the government to invest in power development than to invest (via Nacional Financiera and the Bank of Mexico) in many lines of manufacturing development. In the present stage of Mexico's economic development,

hydroelectric power occupies a basic position.

The issue just raised about power is a special case of a larger issue in the Mexican economy, namely, that of keeping the various branches of the economy roughly in balance as industrialization goes on. There is real danger that manufacturing development will be pushed forward, by both private enterprise and the government, more rapidly than is warranted by rates of expansion elsewhere in the economy. By far the most important lag likely to occur is in the expansion of the domestic market. Back of this lies the difficult job of commercializing, rationalizing, and extending the geographic scope of Mexican agriculture, in order to create buying power in the rural population. The growth of a mass market in Mexico promises to be slow. The habits and ways of life of a people are not remade overnight, even under the most favorable conditions.

The other developments in which significant lags are likely to appear are the improvement of means of transportation (especially the building of a network of secondary roads, but also the rehabilitation of the railway system), the construction of hydroelectric power projects, and the training of laborers, technicians, and managers for industrial enterprises.

The most immediate and most striking expression of bottlenecks and lags in the industrialization process will appear in the form of inflationary pressure. The inflationary whirl which Mexico has experienced since the price level began to climb during the war has already created serious social tensions. It is becoming increasingly apparent to the government administration that these tensions must not be allowed to get worse. The Mexican people have already been badly demoralized by price dislocations. Further inflation, therefore, is likely to cause a serious reduction in working efficiency, as well as a tightening of social and political tensions to a degree previously unknown.

The fact that the Mexican government

has become so sensitive to inflation suggests that more will be done in the future to eliminate inflationary pressures than has been done in the past few years. One of the obvious ways for the government to do this is to reduce public investment and spending, and a certain amount of reduction in the next few years does seem inevitable. Another important measure would be one calculated to slow up the rate of new industrial development by refraining from giving financial support and tax exemptions to new firms. The objective of this policy would be to cut down sharply on the building of new factories, not to interfere with those which have already been started. In addition to reducing the inflationary impact of new investment, this policy would have the advantage of enabling the industrial firms that have got under way in the past few years to consolidate and strengthen their position. Feverish industrialization of the sort Mexico has been going through militates against such consolidation because extreme shortages arise in certain kinds of labor and technical personnel, in fuel and power, and in transportation facilities.

It must be admitted that the odds are against the adoption of a government policy which would drastically curb the rate of new industrial development. High officials of the Mexican government, including President Alemán and the ministers of Finance and National Economy, influential businessmen, such as those whom I have called the New Group, and leaders of organized labor are all convinced that industrialization is the best means to achieve economic and social progress in Mexico. The acceptance of this point of view has led to the belief that industrialization is a substitute for further agrarian reform, and also that immediate industrial development is more important than agricultural development. No administration leader would say that Mexico can get along without a comprehensive agricultural program. But that is not the issue. The main question is which branch of the economy is going to

be regarded as the more important, and the tendency nowadays is to give the preference to industry.

Rather than sacrifice industrial development, therefore, it is likely that the government will take steps, first of all, to cut its outlays and investment in other fields. The agricultural program will probably suffer retrenchment in several branches, such as the subsidizing of the use of farm machinery, agricultural credit, agricultural education, and irrigation. Similarly, it is likely that hydroelectric power development and secondary-road construction will be curtailed, once a policy of reducing government expenditures has been decided upon.

As suggested above, the wiser policy would be to effect a sharp reduction in the rate of industrial development, and to carry out the basic developmental work in agriculture, irrigation, reclamation, power amplification, and road construction as fully as possible. These are not only desirable per se, but they are fundamental for a healthy industrialization of Mexico.

What is needed in Mexico at the present time is perhaps best described as economic planning. This does not mean the building of a rigorously controlled economy, but rather the drawing up of an order of priorities, first of all for each field of development, and then for all fields combined. Projects to be carried out by government investment would obviously be incorporated in such a plan. But it must go beyond this and provide machinery for influencing the decisions of private investors. To discourage new enterprises is not especially difficult, although it may cause irritation in industrial and financial circles. The Mexican government has at its disposal various weapons, notable among which are the following: import controls, which can be used to discriminate against the importation of equipment needed by certain industries; financial controls through qualitative as well as quantitative regulation of bank credit; the law of industry saturation; withholding of tax-exemption privileges; withholding of tariff protection. Legal changes might be necessary in order to make effective use of some of these measures, especially the control of bank credit.

Ever since the Avila Camacho administration started the industrialization drive in Mexico about 1941, there has been much talk of the government's "plan of industrialization." Scarcely an official address has been made on an economic subject without reference to such a plan or program. This, however, should not be taken literally. There has been no plan of industrialization, in any meaningful sense. The only governmental plan has been to encourage private investors, both Mexican and foreign, to build new industrial plants. The government has given aid, by means of tax exemptions and financial support via Nacional Financiera and the Bank of Mexico, but it has not given direction to the industrialization process. For the most part the government has ratified and reinforced the investment decisions made by private enterprise. It has hardly shown initiative in urging private enterprise to undertake industrial developments which are especially needed. But even the will to do this would not have been enough, for it would have been essential, first of all, to know what was needed, and this could have been determined only by drawing up some kind of a plan.

Only in those lines of development where the government acts entirely or largely on its own has planning been engaged in. The Federal Electricity Commission, for example, is carrying out a ten-year program of power expansion drawn up in 1943. The National Irrigation Commission, now succeded by the Ministry of Water Resources, has also done work of a long-range planning character. But planning in such particular fields falls far short of a comprehensive program of national economic development in which, for example, the expansion of industry would be brought into approximate relation with the rate at which additional electric power can be made available.

One [line of thought] . . . frequently encountered in Mexico nowadays is the belief that Mexico finds herself in a position comparable to that of the United States about a hundred years ago, when this country stood at the threshold of her great phase of industrial development. This is indeed an unhappy analogy. The remarkable economic expansion of the United States after 1850 involved three related developments which mutually promoted and strengthened one another — the commercialization of agriculture, the building of a railroad network, and the growth of manufacturing. Perhaps Mexico can approximate such a pattern of related developments in time, when the institutional and other obstacles . . . have been overcome.

But two principal conditions which also favored the economic advance of the United States after 1850 cannot apply in Mexico. One was the enormously rich agricultural resources which were opened up in the interior of the United States in the nineteenth century. The coastal plains of Mexico hold some promise for the future, but they are not in the same class with the Mississippi Valley as a base upon which to build a flourishing economy. The second condition was given by the great economic advance of the world as a whole (in particular, in the industrialized areas) after the middle of the nineteenth century, and by the comparative freedom of commerce which characterized the period 1850–1914. The nature of economic development in the United States, and its pace, were strongly affected by a favorable world environment.

These observations about the experience of the United States suggest the importance of realizing that Mexico is poor in resources for rounded economic development and that world economic conditions are uncertain and undependable. Nor will these international conditions improve rapidly. The future of Mexico's mineral exports is by no means assured in the kind of world economy likely to prevail, and therefore the outlook of Mexico for importing the machinery and equipment needed in industrialization is a clouded one.

These two basic facts about Mexico's resources and the uncertain world economic situation reinforce the reasons already given for the need of a basic plan in working toward the industrialization of the country. Mexico must try to make the maximum use of her slender human and physical resources in a difficult world situation. Mexico cannot afford the luxury of a completely planless development, as the United States could in the nineteenth century.

In some degree the industrialization process is bound to be painful. Economic and social dislocations cannot be prevented. But a modest amount of planning by the government, to give direction to the process and to keep the rate of industrial development in line with other branches of the economy, and especially with the capacity of the market to absorb manufactured goods, will keep the pains of readjustment as a minimum. Such planning, of course, cannot be infallible. Errors of judgment will be made. But the greater error would be for the government to refrain from mapping out a broad program of economic development, leaving the industrial fate of the country entirely to the decisions of private firms.

Mexico seems to have reached the point where her manufacturing capacity for most industrial products promises to outrun the purchasing capacity of her market. In the absence of planning, this discrepancy is destined to grow and to aggravate all the dislocations and problems of industrialization. The emergence of a significant amount of excess capacity will add to the pressure, already strong, for tariff protection. There will be an insistent demand for the government to continue and extend tax-exemption privileges beyond the generous limits allowed by the present law, and also to provide larger amounts of credit to industrial firms — in effect, to maintain a partly unsound industrial structure at public expense. Inflationary tendencies will be worsened. Rather than take measures to reduce drastically the rate of industrial development, the government, in combating an increasingly acute inflationary problem, is likely to make large cuts in its expenditures for agricultural improvement, irrigation, roads, and hydroelectric power. This action will tend to magnify further the discrepancy between Mexico's industrial capacity and the purchasing power of her people.

Mexico has started an industrial revolution destined to go far and to transform the economic and social life of the country. There will be no turning back. The process will go on. In a generation, say, it will have culminated in the sense that the economic and the social structure will differ radically from anything that Mexico has had in the past. To make industrialization as costless and as painless as possible for the Mexican people while that stage is being reached, should be a major concern of the Mexican government. Right now it is essential for the government to take stock, to examine the implications and potential dangers of current rates of development in the various branches of the economy, and to decide whether it should be more selective in promoting industrial development than it has been in the past several years. In short, the government must face the question whether the rate of industrial development should be reduced substantially until the rest of the economy has sufficiently developed to support it. This is the vital economic question in Mexico today.

Industrialization Will Be a Calamity

FRANK TANNENBAUM

Frank Tannenbaum, Professor of History at Columbia University, has probably devoted more of his professional energies to a study of Mexico than has any other United States scholar. His deep sympathy with the Mexican Revolution and with the people of Mexico pervades all his works. In what he perceived to be a shift of emphasis from agricultural reform to industrial development, Tannenbaum saw all the elements of deep tragedy, and the optimism that his earlier works demonstrated had waned by the time he wrote this selection.

A SMALL, industrial-worker upper class, not more than twenty per cent of the total population, is being developed, cut off from the mass of people, producing a relatively narrow range of products at high cost and of poor quality, to be distributed among its own numbers — leaving the rest of the people no better equipped, perhaps less competent, than they were before to secure an access to the benefits of industrialism. It may be argued that this is the only condition under which Mexican manufacturing can come into being. This may be true, but it is equally true that this is not going to achieve the purpose broadcast when the movement was initiated. It may, in fact, throw additional doubt upon the validity of the program itself.

In the meantime the urban population is in a position to absorb any additional gain from the newer industrialism, leaving the rural population as poor as they were before in terms of real income, if not poorer. The situation contains the elements of tragedy, and it cannot be that Mexican labor leaders are entirely unaware of what is implicit in the program. If the agricultural workers really become self-conscious and organized, they may well impose upon Mexico a government attentive to their economic as well as to their political needs — and their economic needs are for low-priced industrial goods in great abundance. But the agricultural population is not yet self-conscious in that sense, and their leaders are still city folk with little understanding of the real problem.

Except low-priced industrial goods, clothing, shoes, tools, and services, the things the city has to offer are of little moment to the country folk; but industry is not pointed toward the mass of hungry consumers in the rural areas. There is no important rural market, and the present industry cannot create it, partly because the poor soil and the ancient agricultural tradition impede any rapid change. The Revolution has added to the size of the urban communities, has increased the middle class, and has created for the first time a native bourgeoisie with all of the appetites of a young capitalist class ambitious for gain in a world where gain is not to be had except from government favors or from the agricultural population. . . .

Economically the rift between the urban and the rural population remains, and is perhaps just as serious as it was before, though it is hidden by the over-all reconstruction effort of the Revolution. The day will come, however, when the Revolution will be over and the internal schism will stand out clearly and remain as largely unremediable as it was before.

In addition to the conditioning features of the trade-union regulations and the tariff, there are a thousand and one government rules prescribing investment and the rights of ownership and determining the kinds of industry that may be developed. These policies are part of the impact of the Revolution, but even more are the result of imbibing theories and ideas neither related to the Mexican milieu nor applicable to its needs. They have proven attractive because of their simplicity and seeming universality. The present-day leaders of Mexico, under the influence of these ideas, have reared a superstructure of governmental regulation that threatens to topple the economy it would order.

The pleasant notions of a planned economy may have their talking-points in a complex industrial society, where the intricacies of the going concern are beyond the ken of the political theorist and are too contradictory for simple political management. An "old" economy, encrusted with tradition, lacking in resiliency, and showing evidence of being incompetent to maintain the older standards of life for a stationary population, may, in despair, turn to "planning" for a solution. These extensive controls may be suited to an economy with a stationary or declining population, in which the emphasis is upon security, keeping the wealth that has already been created and seeing that it is properly distributed. It is not, in terms of past industrial experience, a system for the increase of new wealth, especially a speedy increase such as is demanded by a rapidly expanding population.

What Mexico needs is an increase in the rate of capital accumulation, for only thus can it hope to have a growing average annual real income. If it would not remain poor, or become poorer, then the rate of capital accumulation must increase with sufficient rapidity to provide for the increase in consumer goods and services and thus improve the present level of well-being for both the present and the growing population. . . .

It is one of the cardinal beliefs of the present leadership that the government must intervene to protect Mexico against the foreign interest and even more, to stimulate and direct the industrial and economic development of the country. To this end a long and many-sided series of activities has been fostered, and numerous official and semiofficial institutions have been created. In fact, as stated earlier, the government is involved directly or indirectly, through semiofficial agencies operating with government credit, with governmental personnel, and in conformance with some governmental objective, in almost every economic enterprise in the country.

The central agency in this undertaking is the Nacional Financiera, S.A., first organized with 20 million pesos in 1934. It has since developed into a complex and many-sided institution, operating with large public and increasing private funds, and assuming a directing, perhaps a dominating, position in the guiding of Mexico's industrial development. Its operations are a combination of activities and powers that might be compared to the United States Reconstruction Finance Corporation, the Securities and Exchange Commission, and an investment trust under governmental auspices. In addition it is the leading instrument for floating government bonds. It also intervenes actively in the market, in support of both public and "private" issues. . . .

The government-sponsored and stimulated industrial enterprises are . . . setting the pattern of a high initial cost, justified on the ground that it is developing a private market for such industrial issues. We are told that on December 31, 1944, the Nacional Financiera had outstanding more than 204 million pesos in paper, floated mostly during the previous two years. Of this amount, ninety per cent had been taken up by approximately one thousand individuals. This is considered a most flattering result.

It is an interesting question in terms of public policy whether publicly promoted industrialization, paying high interest rates and offering a guaranteed investment of eight per cent, placed in the hands of a thousand individuals, is a flattering affair. It must be remembered that these industries are protected by a high tariff and, if the tariff is not sufficient, by the prohibition of imports of competing products through a system of import controls. It would seem dubious economic policy to raise the cost of living for an entire nation for the benefit of an industrial structure in which the few shareholders are an infinitesimal part of the population, specially protected against loss by the resources of the government itself, and whose holdings, by a decree of February 12, 1946, enjoy the same immunities from taxation, if devoted to the promotion of industrial production, as the bonds issued by the federal government.

That may, in fact, prove to be industrialization at a price greater than the economy of the country can long sustain. In addition, these activities have given justification for the government's direct participation in the minutest industrial affairs of the country, have greatly extended the powers of the bureaucracy, and have raised the issue of the future relations of these industries, governmentally sponsored and controlled, with organized labor in Mexico, which is also governmentally sponsored and largely controlled. Some day the government may have to choose between its guaranteed financial commitments to the holders of the bonds and stocks under its auspices and the demands of the workers. How such an issue can be resolved, except by an increase in prices, remains to be seen. What has happened is that the government has in a short time moved from the political to the economic sphere, to become the arbiter of the Mexican economy. But this change may have complicated rather than eased the industrial development of the nation. . . .

[A] seemingly conservative estimate of eleven to twelve billion pesos of new capital equipment is prerequisite for any exten-

sive industrialization. Mexico's record with foreign loans and investments is not conducive to optimism on the part of prospective lenders. Nor can it be assumed that new devices such as the Export-Import Bank or the new World Bank can profoundly alter this situation. Without the loans the industrialization cannot take place, because Mexico does not have the resources to supply these needs by itself. Nor are Mexican economists unaware of the issues at stake. The *Revista de la Economía* called attention to these contradictions within the Mexican economy when, on August 31, 1946, it said:

We lack the basic investment that would facilitate the development of manufacturing industries for the diversification of our economy. We have no transportation, we have no electricity. We have no irrigation, and we lack the capital that would make it possible for us to make these basic investments by ourselves.

This large investment, a minimum of between ten and eleven billion pesos, is a preliminary condition for the industrialization of Mexico. A competent railway system, sufficient hydroelectric power, a completed program of irrigation, are the prerequisites for the kind of economic program now envisioned. This investment would not in itself contribute materially to the expansion of Mexican exports and would not, therefore, provide the large amounts of international exchange required for the servicing of these new commitments. They could come only from the growth of a wide and complex manufacturing industry. But such new manufacturing plants would in their turn have to draw heavily upon foreign capital, imported raw materials, skills, and machinery, which in turn would have to be paid for by the increasing exports.

Conditions in Mexico are not favorable for a manufacturing program large enough to pay for both the initial basic capital equipment and the factory development. The country's resources are too narrow and badly structured. Even if the initial foreign investment could be had, it is extremely doubtful if it could be converted into manufactures on a scale sufficient to provide the additional exports essential to the program. If the cost of the investment cannot be serviced — that is, if amortization, repair, and replacement cannot be provided for out of the earnings of these investments — the developments will ultimately deteriorate like the railroads. *And this result is independent of any governmental policy.* Expropriation is no answer to the problem. The new investment must amortize and maintain itself by a continuous flow of new investments for repair, replacement, and expansion, or it must deteriorate. Mexican experience is more than eloquent upon this point.

The conclusion is obvious. The proposed program of large-scale investment for capital equipment as a basis for the growth of an industrial society can be achieved only by assuming a burden of cost greater than the country can support. If the Mexican government wishes to meet the basic issue confronting it — that of finding a means of livelihood for its rapidly increasing population — it will have to devise an alternative program, one more consonant with Mexican realities, and one that it can carry out with greater freedom from dependence upon foreign loans and investments.

I recognize that this will seem a policy of despair; but unless some such alternative program is developed, the conditions in Mexico will within a generation or so be well-nigh desperate. Many Mexicans, and some but by no means all of the professional economists, will reject this conclusion. It will be infinitely better for Mexico, if it turns its eyes to Switzerland and Denmark rather than to the United States as a model and seeks to find a way out on a local, parochial basis in thousands of little communities, adapting to them all of what modern science and skill can make available for the needs of the little community without making it increasingly dependent upon a national market. There is no virtue in flooding these little towns with poor products from factories at high cost

when they can make most of the things they require in their own villages and neighborhoods, with their own hands, by their own arts, and make them beautiful and strong and serviceable. There is no virtue in destroying the Mexican rural community. It is the best thing Mexico has; that is where its strength and resiliency lies. The Revolution proved that certainly.

What Mexico needs is an enrichment of its local communities for increased agricultural production and an increase in the variety and quality of the locally produced handicraft goods sufficient for the local needs and for export as well. *It really needs a philosophy of little things.* The Mexican rural school was that in its beginning, and upon that beginning it ought to build. There ought to be a great emphasis upon little dams, not merely for small-scale irrigation, but also as means for the development of small lakes. With comparatively little effort tens of thousands of small one- or two-hectare ponds and lakes could be built, and built by the villages themselves, without too much overhead, supervision, or direction. Each of these ponds, in addition to all other ends it would serve, could easily become a project for fish-farming, now sufficiently well developed to be taken over by any community that has even the tiniest running brook. Mexico ought to take over and expand the program developed by the state of Missouri. It has been established that an acre pond will supply six hundred pounds of fish annually with a little care and a small expense.

Wherever possible the internal-combustion engine, especially if it is adapted to fuels other than oil (something in the immediate offing), the small electric windmill, or the small hydroelectric plant to serve a given community and its inhabitants ought to be developed.

More important than any of these, perhaps, is the possible adaptability of hydroponics for the growing of potatoes, corn, and other vegetables, which can be easily grown under this system. In Mexico two, three, and for certain items four crops a year could be grown under this method, and it could have almost universal application. In view of the fact that most of the population eat little meat and are not dependent upon wheat, this effort would quickly repay, many times over, the energy put into it. Again, it is something that each village, no matter how small, or even each family, could carry out if the needed chemicals could be procured, and these, from all the evidence, could be produced in Mexico.

The art of making compost ought to be taught in every rural school and in every village. Every effort ought to be made to increase the cultivation of fruit and nut trees of all varieties, not on large plantations, but in every village, in each school ground, and in each man's private yard; and, with it, all of the possible uses of each fruit or nut ought to be developed and taught.

The local crafts and the materials used in their manufacture ought to be studied and improved. Each community ought to be bent in the direction of developing the local resources to make them contribute all they possibly can to the benefit of the local community.

All of this, and a thousand other things, such as seed selection, local sanitation, animal-breeding, and bee-keeping, ought to be developed. To do this would require ten to twenty thousand young men and women trained in the local arts, special skills, and specific sciences adaptable to such a program. They would have to be devoted to their task as the missionaries of old were, and give themselves over completely to redeeming Mexico from the threat of an eroding soil and a growing population.

I must confess to myself with sorrow that both the zeal and the faith have largely departed from Mexico and a mood of cynicism has taken hold of the country, especially in the cities from which the original impulse for such a program would have to come. The city folk — especially in Mexico City, and particularly the government employees who live there — would have it otherwise. They would make big plans, procure large foreign funds, organize great industries, discover some magic in "industrialization," and have a national economy served by a national market at any cost, even if in their hearts they suspect that it is chiefly a dream, which, because of inadequate resources, cannot be realized. But the ideal of bigness is on them, and they will copy and make plans for the impossible even if the Mexico they love must be sacrificed to their notion of "progress."

There is nothing in this proposal that would deny both the need and the possibility of industrial development in Mexico. The extent and the character of such economic expansion, however, can be revealed only by time and experience. An industrial system is a matter of growth and cannot be improvised. Only experience will show what can be done in a country with limited resources, insufficient capital, lack of industrial skill and of the "sixth sense" that comes only with time, not to mention the handicap of a population that by tradition, habit, and attitude is psychologically far away from the "factory hand." It remains to be proved that all of these handicaps can be overcome in a day by government intervention, and it remains yet to be proved that government intervention will in itself not become an impediment to the rapid industrialization of Mexico. It will remain to be proved — for to date Mexico has had past investments in railroads, oil, streetcars, public utilities, telephones and telegraphs, and a thousand other things developed before the recent policies were adopted — that the new policy can do as well as the old or that it can even retain the old services in usable form. I need merely refer to the railroads.

This is not an argument against the present policies. It is merely to point to the fact that these policies are on trial and still have to prove themselves. Even if they do, under the best of conditions they cannot and will not meet the needs of the country if the emphasis is going to be on industrialism for the purpose of a great internal market and a great export industry. If Mexico were wise, Mexican industry would be accepted as a supplement to an agricultural economy, and the emphasis would be upon the marvelous energy and cohesive powers of the rural community. It would use the community to the fullest extent and invigorate it by bringing to it the skills and techniques modern science has made possible for the little place. Mexico, I am convinced, can reach its full-est cultural and economic development only by adopting a policy inherent in its very genius: that of enriching the local community. Any plan that would destroy the vitality of the Mexican rural community is bound to prove tragic in its consequences and repeat the slums of an earlier industrialism without holding out the promise of the increased output that will give employment and sustenance to the fifty or sixty million people who will have to be fed by the end of the century if the present rate of growth continues, as it probably will, during the next two generations.

Mexico Must and Will Industrialize

MANUEL GERMÁN PARRA

Manuel Germán Parra, one of Mexico's most distinguished economists, was cut to the quick by Professor Tannenbaum's pessimism regarding Mexican industrial development, but he paid Mr. Tannenbaum the supreme compliment of devoting an entire book to a refutation of his basic points. It should be noted that Germán Parra repeats an analogy which Sanford Mosk criticized in his work, Industrial Revolution in Mexico, four years earlier: that Mexico is at the same point of economic development as was the United States a hundred years earlier.

THE latest book which Professor Frank Tannenbaum has written expounds a thesis and pursues a purpose. The thesis consists of affirming that our country neither can nor should be an industrial nation. It cannot because it will not be allowed to do so by its economic structure, which corresponds to that of a predominantly agricultural country, demonstrated by the following characteristics: first, the great majority of the population is engaged in agricultural work; second, the poverty of the inhabitants prevents them, in the majority of cases, from consuming industrial articles; third, we are a nation which principally exports raw products and imports manufactured products; fourth, our industry is an artificial monopoly, established under the shelter of excessive customs protection, which produces expensive articles of poor quality and which enriches a minority composed of factory owners and laborers at the expense of the rest of the population, particularly the rural workers; and fifth, industrialization is bringing about a very rapid increase in the population, which is concentrating in urban centers and which is increasing more quickly

From Germán Parra, La Industrialización de México (Mexico, 1954), pp. 35–40, 185–196. Reprinted by permission of Universidad Nacional Autonoma de Mexico. [Editor's translation.]

than the increase in agricultural production indispensable to feed it. But even if Mexico could become an industrial nation it should not, because in so doing it would lose the most valuable asset it has, that which gives it its essential character: the small rural community.

As for the purpose which Professor Tannenbaum pursues, it is an attempt to convince us that all countries in the world are divided into two great categories: those nations born to be industrial and those peoples whose destiny it is to be always agricultural. Mexico belongs, according to the author, to this second group, and not only should not continue trying to industrialize but, on the contrary, must reaffirm its character as a rural nation. This implies leaving the road to urbanization and returning to the epoch in which the nation was an aggregate of small farming communities; in cancelling the great manufacturing industry and returning to the era of the artisan during which every locality made, with its own hands, all the needed articles; in abolishing the national market and re-establishing a market regimen in which each community consumes the products it produces. But this return to the field and to agriculture, to artisanship and local commerce would not, in the judgment of the professor whom we are discussing, constitute a major setback, but an enormous advance, because with its surplus agricultural production the country could buy abroad all those materials necessary to furnish the small communities with the latest conquests of civilization. Thus, and only thus, would Mexico be able to reach its full economic and cultural development.

We propose to demonstrate, in this study, that Professor Tannenbaum's thesis is completely false, and that his purpose could not be more perverse. His thesis is false because it is not certain that Mexico neither can nor should be an industrial nation. It certainly could be, for universal historical experience proves that there do not exist the two categories of countries: those that are and must be always industrial, and those that are and must be always

agricultural; rather there are those which have left off being agricultural and have been converted to industrial nations, and those which have not initiated such transformation or are now in the process of it. Because world economic evolution attests to the fact that it is not true that a country, by the sole condition of being predominantly agricultural, is unable to become an industrial nation; all the industrial nations, including in the very first place those which have arrived at the highest peak of economic progress, have previously been agricultural countries, as agricultural as our country is today and even much more so at certain stages of their development. And Mexico certainly should become industrial, because industrialization is historically the only known road for a country to achieve its fullest economic and cultural development. The theory that a nation can be, at one and the same time, a rural nation and rich, an agricultural nation and advanced, a nation of artisans and prosperous, is under the best of circumstances a bucolic utopia that historical reality itself refutes. As for the assertion that if we industrialize we would lose that which we have of greatest value and that we would sap the strength from our very nature, we must consider it to be, if made in good faith, a romantic bias inasmuch as our national character must be, in each age of our history, nothing more than a product of the level we have reached in our material and cultural evolution.

Since Professor Tannenbaum is a North American, and since in giving his opinion concerning the industrialization of our country he has done nothing less than compare it tacitly with his own, we are going to prove that the case of the United States demonstrates precisely, better than any other, the very contrary of that which he sustains. We are going to prove that North America was one of the most agricultural of nations in the world and that it was able to convert itself, nevertheless, into one of the most industrialized people of the earth; that its economic structure had, over a century ago, the same characteristics that Mexico now has and that, nevertheless, it now possesses precisely the opposite traits. We are going to prove, in effect, that also in the United States the great majority of the population worked in agriculture; that too the poverty of its people prevented, on the part of the majority, the consumption of industrial articles; and that it too was primarily an exporter of raw materials and an importer of manufactured products; that its industry too appeared to be an artificial monopoly established under the shelter of excessive customs protection, which produced expensive articles of poor quality, apparently in order to enrich a minority composed of factory owners and laborers at the expense of the rest of the population, especially the rural; and that too its industrialization brought about a very rapid increase in population which concentrated in urban centers and which increased, for a short time, more rapidly than the agricultural production necessary to feed it. And regardless of all this, in the United States of today the great majority of the population works in non-agricultural activities; the wealth of its inhabitants, regardless of the inequalities of individual incomes, permits them to be consumers of industrial articles; the nation is predominantly an exporter of manufactured products and importer of raw materials; industry is the activity in which more than any other people work, and produces inexpensive articles of good quality which are consumed by the entire nation, including those who live in the countryside; and agricultural production destined to feed the population is increasing faster than the population itself. . . .

The conclusion at which we arrive is that Mexico finds herself at a level of material development similar to that which the United States had achieved toward the end of the first half of the 19th century; that is, that between the economic structures of the two countries there is an evolutionary difference equivalent to a hundred years.

History, fortunately, cannot be reversed. Mexico cannot come to be a more rural nation than it now is, nor should it so become. And, on the contrary, even though it perhaps should not become so, Mexico will become an industrial nation. The industrialization process operating among us is not a product of the economic policy followed by the governments of the past, but, quite the reverse, the economic policy is but a reflection of the industrial revolution which, in turn, is influencing it. Furthermore, the industrialization process taking place in Mexico is not a peculiar and isolated phenomenon, but forms an integral part of an event of universal character which has been transforming the world since the Middle Ages, and which has successively appeared in different countries and from which have sprung the economic, social, political and cultural conditions which have determined its direction. The Mexican industrial revolution is a local phase of the world industrial revolution. For this reason it is impossible to detain it, suspend it or prevent it, even though Professor Tannenbaum tries to convince all Mexicans that it would be wise for us to be de-industrialized and de-urbanized.

For this reason the new theory of the Mexican Revolution which he sketches, but does not develop, in his latest book is also false; this theory attempts to separate, in order to put them in opposition, the agrarian and the industrial revolutions of Mexico. According to this thesis the agrarian revolution represents the most consistent realization of the Mexican revolution because the rural community is the very essence of our country. On the other hand, the industrial revolution constitutes a form in which the revolution is denatured. This conviction is fixed in the author's thinking when he demands that the Mexicans "give themselves over completely to redeeming Mexico from the threat of an eroding soil and a growing population," and that which leads him to affirm with reproachful melancholy:

I must confess to myself with sorrow that both the zeal and the faith have largely departed from Mexico, and a mood of cynicism has taken hold of the country, especially in the cities from which the original impulse for such a program would have to come. The city folk — especially in Mexico City, and particularly the government employees who live there — would have it otherwise. They would make big plans, procure large foreign funds, organize great industries, discover some magic in "industrialization," and have a national economy served by a national market at any cost, even if in their hearts they suspect that it is chiefly a dream, which, because of inadequate resources, cannot be realized. But the ideal of bigness is on them, and they will copy and make plans for the impossible, even if the Mexico they love must be sacrificed to the notion of "progress."

The industrial revolution would signify, thus, a treason to the agrarian revolution, and, therefore, to the Mexican Revolution. But nothing is further from the truth. The agrarian revolution and the industrial revolution in Mexico are not two antagonistic acts, but rather two aspects of the same phenomenon. The agrarian revolution had and continues to have as its object the destruction of the enslaving and feudalistic system under which the country lived, so that it could establish capitalism. The industrial revolution has as its final end the installation of the capitalistic regimen in the length and breadth of the land. Either of these two phases could scarcely begin without the other, and certainly they are not in contradiction. Without the agrarian revolution the industrial revolution could not be brought about, and without the industrial revolution the understanding necessary to fulfill the agrarian revolution is lacking. This is not in any sense a peculiarity of our revolution, but an essential feature common to all the revolutions which have been taking place in the last three centuries, from the 1648 English revolution to the 1944 Guatemalan revolution, during which capitalism has been made the predominant social system in the world. None has been consummated without passing through an agrarian revolution and none has fulfilled its objective without having realized an industrial revolution.

The industrial revolution is an advanced stage of the Mexican Revolution, and thus as before, he who opposed the agrarian revolution in Mexico was an enemy of our economic, social, political and cultural development, now he who fulminates against the industrial revolution is an adversary, hidden or open, of our historic evolution.

Every country can become industrialized, that is, transform its natural resources in raw products and elaborate them to produce manufactured articles. But not all have natural resources which will allow them to make their own producer goods, especially machinery, and above all machinery to make more machinery. Those who do not have these raw materials must always buy these goods from those who make them. But those who do have the materials will have to buy such goods only as long as they do not make them themselves. Mexico is in this last class, and Tannenbaum does not dare deny it. On the contrary, he recognizes that Mexico "is better endowed with natural resources than the majority of other Latin American countries." When the author says that "the resources of the country are too limited," he refers clearly and expressly to the scarcity of capital. And in effect, he says, in this insufficiency consists the impossibility of our continuing to industrialize ourselves and the necessity for our resigning ourselves to being an agricultural country. "If foreign capital is not available, then the program of the Mexican government will be indefinitely postponed or be so slowly developed as to be almost imperceptible," he says in one place, and in another he reiterates: "It [Mexico] needs a great deal of foreign capital for primary construction before a sound, large manufacturing development can take place."

But not even by using foreign capital can we industrialize ourselves, according to Tannenbaum, because nobody would want to lend us the capital and because we would have no way of paying back. Regarding the first, it appears as though our reputation was extremely bad when the author wrote his work: "The Mexican economy," he affirms, "proved incapable of servicing its foreign loans and obligations. It has therefore attempted to reduce the proportion of the foreign interest — even by expropriation — because the burden of payments seemed economically beyond the power of the economy to sustain." This is in reality a criticism of the nationalization policy of the Mexican Revolution, which accords very well with the exaggeration which Tannenbaum makes regarding what he solemnly calls "the historical role of foreign capital in the development of modern Mexico." How could we aspire to obtain new investments, if we have been doing nothing more than dedicating ourselves to reducing or eliminating the old? Only ingratitude could have made us forget that it "was from capital accumulated outside of Mexico that the railroads were built, the mines developed, the oil industry brought into being, the hydroelectric power plants constructed, the street railways laid out, and the cities lighted. The telephone, the telegraph, the large commercial establishments, the textile industry, the steel works, the public sanitation and even the larger retail trade in tools, machinery, drugs, and department stores were wholly or partly financed by foreign capital, developed with foreign skill, and serviced by foreign technicians. Without their foreign capital and foreign technical aid Mexico would have remained a wholly primitive, agricultural, and disunited nation. The claim that the price was high may be true; but the capital goods represented by the price paid are what Mexico has to look to as a base upon which to build for the future."

. . . The price that Mexico paid for investments of this type was not *perhaps* high, as he says, but extraordinarily elevated. The struggle of the great foreign enterprises in Mexico, particularly the oil companies, against the movement, the legislation and the government born of the Mexican Revolution, which Tannenbaum relates with such precision, demonstrates that this class of foreign capital was responsible for our country not being able to develop our economy rapidly and freely during the first decades of the revolutionary era.

This, unfortunately, is not the only error from which Professor Tannenbaum suffers. It is not certain that without foreign investment Mexico would have continued to be a completely primitive, agricultural and disunited country. At most, in the same manner in which the author expounds his thesis, nothing would prevent one from extending the generalization to other countries, and to suppose that no nation can blossom without the participation, in a decisive amount, of foreign capital. But then the generalization would be principally applicable to the case of the United States, in whose initial economic development foreign investment had such a major role. But would Tannenbaum venture to insist that his country would have continued to be a completely primitive, agricultural and disunited country, something akin to a confederation of redskin tribes, had European capital not had the kindness to invest in his territory? But even though he would agree to this, could he tell us with what foreign capital England was industrialized? What international investments produced the industrialization of France and the majority of the industrial nations of Europe? Universal historical experience proves that foreign capital is not indispensable for the economic evolution of a country.

The above does not mean, nevertheless, that it would not be useful, or that a country should refuse to accept or even fail to procure foreign capital. On the contrary. Even though foreign capital does not determine the economic development of a nation, it does contribute much to accelerate it, always given that the investment be not made in such a form as to contribute to the contrary. To judge in the abstract whether an investment is good or bad results in a purely scholastic question. It will be good or bad depending upon a multitude of concrete factors which may be summarized thus: it will be useful if foreign capital is put to the service of the country, and hurtful if it makes the country put itself to the service of the foreign capital; it will be desirable if it contributes to the harmonious economic flowering of the nation, and it will be condemnable if it deforms the structure of its economy. In a word, the criterion for judging an investment of foreign capital should consist always not of determining how much it foments economic progress, but the extent to which in practice it guarantees national economic independence and how much it is going to contribute to fortifying that independence.

Mexico could continue to be industrialized in the future without counting on any but her own financial resources, scarce though they still may be. But it cannot be denied that her process of industrialization would be less rapid than if she permitted the investment of those types of foreign capital that would not deform her material development or erode her economic independence. It is false to say that our past policy of nationalization of natural resources was an obstacle to making these investments, because any truly objective observer can prove that the policy did not despoil anyone of his legitimate interests, but that it only prevented our economic and political life from being dictated by norms distinct from its own. The practice of demanding of foreign capital that it collaborate in the economic development of the country, in return for legitimate security and reasonable profits, far from being conducive to economic isolation and political antagonism respecting other nations, will result in the surest base for an international economic cooperation growing steadily firmer. To strengthen all economic relations with other countries, thereby serving to foment our development within the principles of national economic independence, should be the essential postulate in foreign economic policy of our country.

In the next lustrums Mexico will more and more cease to be an agricultural country and will more and more be transformed into an industrial nation. The mortality rate will continue to lower and the population will be increasing more and more rapidly. The division of labor process will more and more diversify production and force the producers to produce less and less for their own consumption and more and more for exchange. Lines of communication and means of transport will multiply more and more. The localities in which the inhabitants live isolated will become dependent upon the national market. The market for industrial articles will increase, and industry will be increasing the number of its factories and absorbing a greater and greater proportion of the rural population. The peasantry will more and more be separated, one part to become modern small proprietors, one part agricultural laborers and a third part — the best of all — industrial laborers. The artisans too will gradually disappear to become a part of the manufacturing industry. The rural communities will more and more be transformed into urban centers. The increasing population will be concentrating in the great cities. The languages and cultures of the indigenous population will be disappearing. A single economy and a single culture will make Mexico a modern nation, intimately linked to the rest of the world. . . .

The best economic policy will be that which has the greatest consciousness of the country's industrialization process and contributes most to its acceleration without a diminution of the harmonious development of the other branches of the economy. It will be that which channels this process within a general and concrete program, of a quantitative character, in which a very precise hierarchy among the distinctive activities is established and which will indicate the limits it would be desirable to reach and investments which would be necessary to direct toward each. The best economic policy will be that which protects the national economy against ruinous foreign competition, but which will force it to become at the same time modernized to improve the quality of its articles and to reduce its cost and prices. It will be that which encourages, along with industrial production, agriculture, silviculture, cattle growing, aviculture, fishing and mining in order to furnish more raw materials; railways, highways and port facilities in order to transport more raw materials and manufactured products; railroads, trucks and ships to carry more merchandize from the centers of production to those of consumption; and oil and electricity to power more factories and more vehicles. The best economic policy will be that which is able to channel the use of credit for the functioning of the most important economic activities, and in proportion to that importance. . . . The best economic policy, in short, will be that which promotes the greatest and most rapid material progress in whatever form, in the briefest possible time, with the greatest economic independence and with the highest standard of living for the people.

VI. POLITICS: THE DEMOCRATIC PROCESS

The Need for Civic Education

A. SILVA VILLALOBOS

A. Silva Villalobos is thoroughly in accord with the basic tenets of the Mexican Revolution, and he is generally in accord with the policy of the revolutionary governments. His "accusation" concerns only those political aspects which keep Mexico from developing into a true democracy. He fears that unless the Mexican people are educated for democracy in some realistic and conscientious way, the great spirit of the Revolution will be dissipated by the apathy of the masses and the opportunism of their leaders.

MEXICAN domestic policy, guided by revolutionary ideas, has given our people the enormous benefits they enjoy today, if we compare the present order of living with that enjoyed in the last years of the past century; this is a well-known and well-studied theme which needs no further examination. A great part of the national patrimony, such as oil, railroads and great stretches of land, have been recovered even though we still do not have the mines. The conquests of syndicalism have brought a notable improvement in the life of the workers, and the agrarian reform has been beneficial for the peasants. In student education a good beginning has been made with the constant increase in educational centers and the formation of an attitude among parents so that students may acquire instruction. Nevertheless, there is something very important, which should be a constant theme in its programs, forgotten by the Revolution: civic education. Of this our public is ignorant.

Such education should be the backbone of our conduct in two principal spheres: that essentially political or electoral, and the daily life of the individual in his acts important to the collectivity.

Respecting the first we can give some history. At the beginning of the Revolution it was necessary to unfurl the banner of *effective suffrage* only as a symbol, for to have converted it into a reality would have been fatal because of the overwhelming clericalism and ignorance of the people. The imposition of some revolutionary groups was necessary in order to launch the rights of liberty and the rights of dignity of labor. But with the passage of time the symbol became the end, and the governments of the Revolution forgot to make it effective. What have these governments done to educate the people in civic affairs, in a fashion so that all citizens are capable of electing their representatives? There has been no program worthy of mention in this respect, and the situation continues to be the same since we all know that the candidacies of public representatives do not come from the public but from the upper official regions, specifically from the president of the republic. Everything is done through the headquarters of the official

From A. Silva Villalobos, *Acusacíon Política* (Mexico, 1958), pp. 1–13. Reprinted by permission of the publisher, Moscos de Metafora. [Editor's translation.]

party, where not even the governors count. To those are left the role, occasionally, of distributing public posts only in their States.

Civic education begins to show, in a very rickety fashion, during the great electoral campaigns but it is not thus, for a few months every six years, that the public should have the means of learning the exercise of their duties and their rights.

It is absolutely necessary to educate the public to prevent suffrage from being made a pernicious myth. Lack of respect for the popular will begins to damage the very conscience of the nation; the imposition of a candidate which forces the public to vote for him is not democracy. And it is generally considered to be inevitable that the candidates of the party in power will win, even though they have neither ability or general support. We are not discussing the parties of opposition, because they have not known how to comply with their responsibilities. The rightists are so slow in their advance toward liberalism that after a hundred years it has not seen the light of day. The leftists cannot take part in the destinies of the country because they would destroy the very interests of the Revolution.

Sometimes the indolence of the public is confused with its civic progress. Our official party has boasted of the unity of the Mexicans and its responsibilities stemming from past elections. The candidacy of Adolfo López Mateos was an extraordinary success, really astonishing, but it hides a great danger. All sectors were willing to have him rule over their destinies. Nevertheless the day will come when it will be discovered that in all sectors there has been the hypocritical notion of taking refuge under his triumphant mantle in order to extract maximum benefits. If to this we add the fact that no social sector of importance dared to put forward a candidate prior to the designation by the official party, the situation is considerably aggravated.

Now, as never before, something intervenes in our electoral contests, something which must disappear: the *cargada*, a political abnormality which today, by its proportions, and through the delegations of powers, threatens to create in the president of the republic the only authority. We all know that in order to resolve any conflict it is necessary to go to the president because other officials never have sufficient power to impose a solution. Every day the centralization of power is greater.

We all know that the candidate of the official party for the presidency of the republic takes into consideration the opinion of some ex-presidents when he is elected. This system, even though foreign to democracy, could pass muster if its only intention were to give the presidency to one who knew how to continue our liberating tradition, but unfortunately its function is to assure respect for the interests of the big politicians — always millionaires — during the coming administration. In this fashion we have been supporting a badly disguised oligarchy. There has thus been created, on the foundation of a popular revolution, a circle of political leaders who have put into effect a calculated rotation in public posts and whose number is renewed in a tiny percentage from people well versed in this system which impedes social and political capillarity.

The concentration of power has a rationale for the official circles: our citizens are still not prepared. How much time does the Mexican public need to become prepared? An eternity unless the governments of the Revolution are dedicated to initiating that preparation. Civic education is not achieved in the schools by lessons about heroes, nor do men learn it by going to commemorations and listening to empty, repetitious and demagogic speeches. Civic education should be the object of a vast plan aimed at creating in the young a feeling of responsibility regarding national problems, so that the destiny which belongs to them is not left to be snatched away by clever politicians. At the moment the educational programs, including that for the preparation of teachers, are far from creating whole men who will be able to act not only professionally but civically.

On the other hand the system of the great electoral campaigns must be modified. During the last election we had the impression that we were offered a commercial product of low quality. Such was the insistence. And this echoes the lack of civic consciousness; the public needs the modern psychological treatment of publicity in order to feel confidence. The leaders know it and have intoxicated the public with López Mateos. They exaggerated the propaganda to the point of nausea in a cachinnation of subterfuge. On a cemetery wall we read: *the dead with López Mateos.*

The campaign speeches are ideologically indecisive and filled with promises concerning little, material things. As always, the politicians sell illusions and the public is accustomed to pay dearly for them. With regard to the last campaign, it is only necessary to take into account López Mateos' first speech. It sketches the national situation very well, but it gives a glimpse of some intentions which are unfavorable to the public. For example, the idea concerning industrialization: "An adequate industry requires the strengthening and the amplification of the capacity to purchase by great sectors of the society in order to allow for large scale manufacturing production." In these terms it is clear that the object is to pursue manufacturing on a large scale, and only as a means to that end is an increase in personal income proposed, and even though these economic factors are correlated, we fear that such a definition could be interpreted as the motto of the great monopolists of other countries. They are able to create necessities in the minds of the individual with the sole object of selling their products, and to increase their economic power at the expense of the masses. Thus understood, industrialization is promising to deposit the wealth in the hands of the oligarchy from which we now suffer and to augment the already well-accented economic differences among the Mexican people.

With regard to man's daily life, public civic education should result in a firm consciousness of responsibility with respect to national problems. To be responsible implies that one should interest himself in common problems and consider the rest of society before taking a personal action which might affect it. The attitude of those who profess an erroneous individualism results in the committing of a theft or a fraud. The desire to take advantage of whatever seasonable opportunity there exists for economic speculation, against which the government of Mexico has had to pass laws, ineffectually, is nothing less than a lack of civic consciousness. The artificial augmentation of prices of the means of subsistence is showing us a strong irresponsibility regarding national problems. . . .

Abuse is the word which has been selected to classify the attitude of these irresponsible people, and our government has had posters put up, in the capital, inviting the citizens to cooperate in the denunciation of such acts. But do these posters fastened on street corners solve a problem of loyalty?

Some organs of service to the public, such as the police or the transport agents, have been converted into its worst enemies thanks to the more and more intolerable *mordida*,[1] also ensconced in public office. To what is this shameful system, which appears to have been a Mexican invention, owed? We insist that it is the product of not having civically educated the public, because in this case too it is working to the prejudice of the majority in order to benefit the particular. If not, in what other manner could we classify the act of an inspector of a factory, for example, in giving in exchange for a *mordida* a clean bill of health to an establishment which does not have the indispensable safeguards for the workers?

Now abuse, *mordida* and other similar situations are owing, individually, to the insufficiency of income at all levels, and for this we can only blame the national

[1] Literally, a *bite*; as here used, petty graft. [Editor's note.]

economy which for historical or international reasons, or because of errors by its leaders, is not in a prosperous condition. This apparently explains the situation, but it nevertheless would not happen if the public were civically educated, because if each citizen felt a responsibility for national problems he could work in accord with the general possibilities and would not attempt to extract for himself the best advantage of a situation at the cost of aggravating the problem. Irresponsibility puts individuals into a part of the problem and not of the society, without considering that farther along they themselves will have to suffer the consequences.

In recent months (this is written in October, 1958) Mexico has suffered some grave events which have paralyzed the life of the country, some such as the strikes by the telegraphers and the railroad workers, and others such as the strikes of the teachers which have so prejudiced the interest of Mexican children, the problems of the petroleum workers, and later still the bellicose attitude of the students in the capital against an increase in the urban transport fares.

All these events are indicating to us the beginning of a discontent whose roots are not now visible but indubitably have great depth in the Mexican public. The deficient political system, the poorly directed economy and the lack of a sense of collectivity create problems which begin to manifest themselves in very diverse ways. We are entering into a period for revising the fruits of the Revolution, perhaps because the results, at first satisfactory, are far from being optimum and the general situation of the country requires a reform of the principles which govern it.

It is not possible to claim, as the moving force for these events, only intervention of agitators with an international political tendency. Only in a propitious ambient do such maneuvers flow, and our government ought to bring this situation to an end immediately, not on the basis of lulling them, but of solving them. Problems of union policy and of increase in salaries

have been the immediate motives of these social movements, which could be a beginning of a class consciousness formed by necessity and not the result of a directed education as it should be. Labor unionism . . . has been converted into a system to sustain a group of leaders who betray the interests of the workers, and at the same time prevents the emergence of new citizens in the sphere of popular political representation. It could be said that the lack of consciousness among the laboring classes is creating in our days a destiny adverse to unionism and threatens the collapse of the conquests obtained by it. Because the movements of which we are speaking are not the conscious and authentic will of the groups, they signify the beginning of a rebellion against the perpetual leaders and the deficient economic situation. And the government of our country must not, through the repression of discontented ones, encourage interests foreign to Mexico to take up the banner for just causes among our citizens. The revolutionary principles should give us a solution. And we should not be afraid to reform or to add to the ideas born in 1910. Revolution has signified for us social justice adequate to the reality, and we must make it effective.

We cannot be in accord with the ideas that the means of resolving this kind of problem is force. This is an easy but dangerous road because it signifies the beginning of tyranny. To confront the discontented groups with armed force is a confession of not knowing how to govern a country which has the prestige of enjoying full liberties. To know how to govern is to maintain, above all else, this gift which our public has gained many times with the lives of its men. When a government employs force to attack a problem it does not resolve it; it multiplies it in the long run. The government of Mexico should understand the country's situation; it should be careful not to expose it to an internal struggle which would only benefit foreign interests.

In these circumstances we should dare

to recall to President Ruiz Cortines his own words: "I am certain that the abuse of civil liberties causes the Republic fewer ills than the most moderate exercise of a dictatorship." And later he threatened: "We live in an epoch in which the velleity of certain political retrogressions are usually paid for with the rigor of a dictatorship." This is true, but the public should not have to pay for the velleities of a government which first gives it guarantees and then takes them away.

Our situation is grave and dictatorship and tyranny really threaten us. Public and government should understand each other so that Mexico does not become a victim of a growth which denies the principles of the Revolution.

Democracy Does Not Exist in Mexico

MANUEL GÓMEZ MORÍN

Partido Acción Nacional, organized in 1939 in opposition to the official Partido Revolucionario Institucional, is the only party of opposition which has been able to maintain itself over the years and the only party, other than PRI, which has had a presidential candidate in every election since 1940. As a party which poses a threat to the continued political monopoly held by PRI, PAN has been consistently subjected to considerable pressure by the official party and by government officials. Manuel Gómez Morín was one of the founders of the party and held a position roughly analogous to that of the Chairman of the National Committee of one of the major parties in the United States when he made the following report to the National Convention on February 25, 1949, concerning the congressional elections of 1948.

IMMEDIATELY after the National Convention of the National Action Party in this city last February, and in fulfillment of the resolutions there passed, the committees of the party began the electoral campaign for deputies to the National Congress. In the various conventions held, candidates from sixty-nine districts in twenty-three states were nominated.

The Party organization and the candidates first and principally undertook to obtain the most efficient possible functioning of the registration offices, and to register the greatest possible number of citizens. In this task they were obstructed by the obstacles systematically erected by the Registry Council and its agents. The Registry Council, in an action which can only be described as deliberate sabotage, devised an absurd territorial division in the establishment of its offices throughout the country, turned over the major portion of these offices to the PRI subordinates or to the employees or dependents of the local bosses, and blocked — to the point of total obstruction — representation by independent parties, particularly National Action, in the formation of the registry.

All the facts of the notoriously criminal activity of the Registry Council — the in-

From Manuel Gómez Morín, *Diez Años de México* (Mexico, 1950), pp. 277–291. Reprinted by permission of Editorial Jus. [Editor's translation.]

credible and deliberate inefficiency, the notorious partiality, the falsifications and the irregularities committed in the registration by virtue of which great numbers of citizens were denied the possibility of exercising their rights and fulfilling their duty, and the thousands of false credentials which were given to agents or candidates of the official party or to the local bosses to allow them to supplant voters — are well known.

To the official party and its candidates these frauds did not appear sufficient to assure their "triumph" at the polls. Therefore the Federal Commission of Electoral Supervision, composed of members of the regime who are public functionaries, turned over the Local Electoral Commissions to the official party, or its agents, or the governors; the local commissions, with even more open partisanship, overrode the justified objections of our commissions and representatives and flouted the law by virtually totally handing over the district committees to the lesser agents of the official party, to the little local bosses masquerading as municipal authorities and, in some cases, to men whose apparent independence was a cover-up for their cowardice and servility.

This surrender of the electoral machinery to men who made it an instrument of contemptible fraud reached its lowest point of disgusting partiality and indecency with the naming of the personnel of the voting booths, which in the vast majority of cases were put into the hands of the basest agents of the PRI and the local bosses.

The commissioners and representatives of this Party complied with their duties in the electoral process. In the impossibility of naming all those who used their posts to defend, with abnegation and valor, the rights of citizens and the basic institutions of Mexico, and inasmuch as this meeting itself is a testimonial of thanks and gratitude to all of them, I will limit myself to mentioning only Roberto Cossio y Cosio, who fought passionately against the ineffi-

ciency of the electoral service, the illegitimate partisanship and the fraud. For the same reason I will limit myself to a mention of the district voting committees of the Ninth and Tenth Districts of the Federal District — and especially those citizens, not members of National Action, who presided over the committees — and those in charge of the voting booths in the Tenth District as well as many of those in the Ninth and Twelfth Districts, as examples of decorum in the fulfillment of a duty and as models of what an electoral system could be if it did indeed guarantee the authenticity of and respect for voting instead of being merely an irresponsible tool for the regime.

The entire electoral machinery, from those in charge of the voting booths to the Federal Commission of Electoral Supervision, did all they could, without even going through the most elemental forms, to mock the election, to impede or restrict the vote, to prevent independent candidates and parties from exercising their prerogatives and fulfilling their duties, to make the proof of these irregularities and abuses impossible, and finally to falsify the balloting itself through the supplantation of voters, the stuffing of ballot boxes or — when all these were insufficient to distort the real result of authentic balloting — the allowing of polling place presidents to abscond with the ballot boxes; in this last maneuver the army was forced to become an accomplice, since the military forces were given an unconditional order to obey the polling place presidents, those thieves of the popular votes.

But even this was not sufficient to conquer the citizens who voted. Then the tallying commissions arrived; sometimes they limited themselves to the certification of notoriously fraudulent votes or the even more fraudulent count of stolen boxes; but on some occasions the commission went so far as to prevent the presence of the presidents of the polling places for the tallying, and on others they saw to it that the genuine votes were not delivered for the tally.

The Electoral College, which under the

absurd existing system is composed of the very authors or beneficiaries of the inefficient service, the falsification of credentials and votes, the stealing of ballot boxes and the farce of the tallying commissions, has proceeded as it has on past occasions; by a curious logic the most irrefutable proofs and the soundest arguments are subordinated to the pressures and internal disputes within the regime.

National Action objected to fifty sets of credentials illegally granted to PRI candidates as victorious, and sustained the undoubted validity of the credentials granted to its candidate in the Tenth District of the Federal District. Of the cases which the Party contested, to date the Electoral College has reviewed forty-four, only four of which have been decided in our favor.

The nature of the debates in the Electoral College is well known. The candidates and the Deputies of the Party have denounced and proved the voting frauds, pledging themselves to defend the rights of citizenship and to point out the illegalities and the grave ills for Mexico deriving from a continuation of the system of voting mockery which bastardizes representation and thereby falsifies or brings to ruin all the other institutions of our public life.

The official majority has justified its decision by limiting itself to the simple negation of the validity of the proofs, and by the constant reiteration of a theme — coined by the regime with fictitious stories about reaction and about the Party's responsibilities for the Conquest, the crowning of Iturbide and the Maximillian Empire — which falsifies the Party's posture. Two lines of argument, presented with a show of intellectual authority by the official majority in these debates, may be pointed out. One affirms that the notarial documents have no probatory value in electoral matters. The other discovers that there are two democracies, one of which is "explicit" with popular mandates and representation deriving from the vote, as happens among superior people, and the other of which is "implicit democracy," "functional," proper

for inferior people such as ours, in which the mandate and representation do not derive from a vote — a mere formality — but from the "permanence" of the great tendencies of the organized masses.

Under Article 97 of the Constitution, which establishes a legal means for defending the suffrage, the National Committee of the Party appealed to the Supreme Court with a request that the high tribunal investigate the acts of violation during the voting — crimes punishable under federal law — committed during the last election. The suit presented the violations and the facts in detailed form, and, moreover, seven memorials were presented in which concrete facts were given which the Supreme Court could have and should have investigated. Against the votes of five members of the Tribunal, and without citing any reason for not taking an action which the constitution leaves to its discretion, the Court decided to abstain from undertaking an investigation which could have been the exercise of one of the highest functions expressly given by the constitution; it thus could have contributed to a broadening of its sphere of competence on an occasion extraordinarily propitious and opportune for doing so without running the risk of being dragged into a party fight. This not only would have contributed to the restoration of violated rights, but also to the definitive extirpation of those methods and procedures which, by subverting constitutional order at its very bases — effective suffrage and genuine representation — weaken and convulse our economy, impede true social reform, and close the road to the nation's firm and organic progress.

The federal government has in its possession numerous charges concerning the electoral crimes committed. It would not be difficult for the Attorney General's office to investigate these and other charges which will be presented along with copious data and proofs. It will remain with the Attorney General's office to comply with its duty or not, as was the case with the Court, as it has been with the Electoral

College, and as it was with the entire electoral machinery and the regime which constituted it. In its hands rests the possibility of giving Mexico the inestimable value of applying strong legal sanctions to those who commit electoral fraud, and most especially to those who, charged with the responsibility of guarding the right of a free and orderly manifestation and the respect for the will of the citizenry, have instead — and in full consciousness of the immense damage to Mexico — disorganized the electoral service, violated the letter and the spirit of the law, and made of the suffrage a new and impardonable mockery by putting all the economic, administrative, juridical, and social resources of the government at the service of that illegitimate counterfeit of a party called the PRI.

In Nuevo León, National Action participated in local elections by nominating candidates for governor, state deputies and all the electoral judicial positions. Antonio L. Rodríguez directed a brilliant campaign, in which the people of Nuevo León, the militant members of the Party, and the local boards, following the magnificent lead of the municipal elections in the state some months before, demonstrated their civic capabilities and defended the rights of the citizens to resolve collective problems, to designate their representatives and public officials, and to take into their hands the common destiny.

The regime realized, after the municipal elections in which National Action candidates triumphed, that the gang they had supported through the use of local bosses for so many years would be unable to resist the new citizen movement. They then decided to make an imposition on a grand scale by sending to Nuevo León a gubernatorial candidate who would ostensibly signalize the possibility of change, and by putting not only the resources of local bossism but the full weight of the federal government at the service of the campaign for the new imposition.

This posture was not sufficient to modify the obvious inclination of the citizenry or to detain the popular movement. [...] garchy which had long ago usu [...] local government therefore accepted [...] changed conditions and with a grotesque mixture of discipline and resentment changed their candidate and their ideological trappings, and extended their arms — not always rejected in spite of their dirtiness — to those groups who previously had been the favorite targets of attack. But the tendered hand which is used to cheat the public is not effective, and the regime which tries to change its method does not hit the mark. Impoverished by its own system of falsification, and by the terror which the simple possibility of a popular vote inspired, the regime was caught in its own system. The public officials, every instrument available to the state and municipal governments, the agencies of federal government, and all those institutions which should have been autonomous were put to the service of the official candidate. The electoral instrumentalities were more openly given to fraud than in the national elections. The Registry Council, the personnel of the voting booths and all the legal instrumentalities designed to protect the suffrage remained in servile subordination to the regime's candidate. The imposition did not depend only on the ordinary methods of electoral fraud, nor on psychological, administrative and fiscal coercion on the citizenry. Convinced that if there were an election it would be adverse, the regime dedicated itself to make an election impossible by impeding the balloting and substituting for it the common fraud of flying squads of spurious voters with cynically fabricated voting documents.

The formal declaration of the official result in the Nuevo Leon election is still pending. The real result has been a new and obvious exhibition of the regime's ineptitude, of the voracious appetite for power which prevents a recognition of the urgent need for substantial and radical reform; reform consisting not merely of a change of some wicked government-imposed bosses by others equally imposed but who appear or promise to be less wicked, but designed to satisfy a just desire for political liberty and to guarantee suffrage and representation as the very cement of public life. The real result, for the public, has been a reaffirmation of the possibility of giving life to democratic institutions, a demonstration that it is the regime itself — that group of men who have usurped authority — which blindly insists on closing the way to orderly and fecund political progress; an indication that there exists in Mexico only that which the lamentable leader of the official majority in the Chamber of Deputies called "implicit democracy" not because the people of Mexico are inferior, but because those who unlawfully retain power are inferior.

The campaigns, too, have made patent the urgency for true electoral reform such as that which National Action has been advocating. Yet during the special session of Congress this demand for reform was sidetracked by a stratagem. And even the normally responsible organs of public information let it pass without being aware of its grave consequences, of the fraud perpetrated.

It is now clear to everyone that a complete and truly citizen's voter registry is the very base of an electoral system, and that it is impossible to have such a registry if the voters are registered only every three years — and this by the manipulators of the imposition with no public opportunity for revision or inspection. The Registry should be permanent, confided to an autonomous, responsible and impartial agency, open to constant public scrutiny by individual citizens and by parties.

And it is equally manifest that the electoral service should not, in its organization and its functioning, be handed over to bodies installed by the regime or the official party; it also must be confided to agencies which have the same characteristics of autonomy, personal responsibility and impartiality, and which are especially competent to give to Mexico the incomparable benefits of a true electoral service, the prime and most important of the national public services.

Finally, it is obvious that certification of electoral results cannot be entrusted to a tribunal made up of those responsible for the electoral frauds. The monstrous system of the Electoral College, in which those acting as judges are a part of the system, should be changed into a true tribunal which, to give more complete guarantees of impartiality and to prevent the creation of political interests and appetites, should have the above characteristics common to all agencies of public service and furthermore should be an impermanent body formed for each election, should be dissolved at the conclusion of each contest, and should be composed of persons who satisfy the requisites of ability, rectitude and independence of criteria, proved by firm antecedents of honor and patriotism.

These are the three central chapters of urgent reform. The modification of the electoral procedure itself and the creation of those resources which would permit the prevention or correction of errors or abuses, before inevitable ills are produced, will be a consequence of and a complement to these basic reforms.

Mexico's Democratic Syndrome

ROBERT E. SCOTT

Robert E. Scott is a Professor of Political Science at the University of Illinois; his *Mexican Government in Transition,* from which the following selection is taken, is the best work available on contemporary Mexican political developments.

GOVERNMENT AND THE INDIVIDUAL

THIS book has attempted to describe the development of systematic, Western-style government in Mexico, even though the transition is not yet complete. . . . One important question does remain to be considered. How well does Mexico's evolving political system serve the individual, whether he participates in one or more of the interest groups which share in the decision-making process or whether he remains outside of the active machinery of policy determining?

This is a significant question in determining the success or failure of the transition toward a Western system of government in any country. As Roy Macridis says,

The test of any system is the opportunities it provides to the individual to live peacefully with his fellowmen, that is, internal security and the development of institutions for the adjustment of individual and group conflict. A political system should provide men with opportunities for employment and economic security as well as for political participation. This means that the system should provide for education and freedom in the widest possible sense of the word — freedom of thought and expression, religious freedom, and freedom of association and political action. Above all, men must be treated by the government on a footing of equality. This means that they should not be differentiated on any basis other than ability and achievement; it also means that no handicaps should be placed for any reason whatsoever upon the potentiality of a man's development.[1]

The fair-minded reader will admit readily that Mexico already has traveled quite a distance along the road to this ideal, but even the most friendly observer, one who identifies emotionally with the hopes, desires, and struggles of the Mexican people, must concede that Mexico's political system has not yet arrived at this stage of perfection. From the viewpoint of a study concerned primarily with the long-range pattern of political development and the gradual evolution of working political institutions for the satisfactory adjustment of individual and group conflicts, however, the vital point is not simply the degree of achievement at this particular moment. Instead, it is found in a question posed earlier in the book — whether the kind of responsible and effective government normally associated with the democratic aspirations of Western man reasonably can be expected to evolve in time. On the basis of what has taken place since 1910, and especially since 1930, I believe that such a political system can be expected to develop in Mexico.

Democratic government, in the Western sense of the term, is a great deal more than

[1] *The Study of Comparative Government* (New York, 1955), p. 62. [Author's note.]

From Robert E. Scott, *Mexican Government in Transition* (Urbana, 1959), pp. 294–304. Reprinted by permission of the University of Illinois Press.

a political idea, or even ideal; as Macridis suggests, it involves the social situation and the economic conditions under which the individual exists, in addition to his political freedom. As such, a democratic political system reflects a whole way of life, in which the normal, daily human activities of the citizens are as important as the operations of formal government agencies. Democracy as a political system cannot long coexist with social or economic inequity and, conversely, a fluid society and viable economy are apt to produce conditions favorable to democratic government, for all human activities and values must be reasonably consistent with each other if stability is to exist in a given society. This does not mean, however, that every country in which social change or economic development is taking place may be classed automatically as a future democracy, for in addition to material conditions, the concept requires the acceptance of a particular set of values by a broad cross-section of the society. Consider the reversals suffered recently by the hopeful democratically inspired governments of the emerging Asian states because of the lack of any commonly shared understanding of what democracy entails. Or consider the alien form, by Western standards, that "people's democracy" takes in the Soviet Union, where the traditional value system supports authoritarianism and orthodoxy at the expense of responsible, representative government and individual freedom in social and economic matters as well as in political activity.

Growing as it does out of the social activities of large numbers of persons, democracy eludes formal or mechanistic definitions; it can be discussed best by means of a working definition that takes into account the action of people and the fluidity of the concept itself. One way to test Mexico's ongoing system of politics for evidence of democratic tendencies is to search for a democratic syndrome; that is, a significantly strong pattern of observable signs and symptoms which characterize democracy, occurring together in sufficient proportions to render any existing nondemocratic characteristics less and less operative, until a diagnosis of effective democracy is possible. Every political system contains some of the elements of democracy, just as it does some nondemocratic factors, so the important fact is not the existence of either but the respective roles they play in the political process; this offers an indication of a trend toward democratic government, if one exists.

As a minimum, Mexico's democratic syndrome must include a degree of limited, responsible, and popular government within a formalized, though not necessarily written, constitutional system. To operate successfully, such government presupposes relatively widespread public agreement on basic social and political values, so that the limits of governmental action prescribed by the political system are acceptable to and enforced by a large enough part of the citizenry to assure orderly administration. This, in turn, requires that the largest possible portion of the people be politically aware and well enough educated to demand effective action in matters of their concern. Corollary to this active popular role in government, and an absolute requirement for democracy, is the need both under the law and in the popular mind for recognition of the essential equality of all human beings and at least some acceptance of the fundamental dignity of the individual in relation to other individuals.

In testing for Mexico's democratic syndrome, we must consider carefully the political process in which these general factors operate, being equally careful to measure their role in that process in the currency of the country. That is, we must recognize that we are studying social institutions and political habit patterns which have meaning in Mexico rather than in some other country with different values, ideologies, and political culture. Taking this into account, we must seek to determine whether the political process operates in an environment of broadly enough shared values and understandings of the role and function of government for the minority to accept the decision of the majority and for the government in power to offer a high degree of toleration to the opposition. If most politically active persons, no matter which party or faction they belong to, are loyal to the general concepts of the political and constitutional system, chances are that the usual mechanisms of democratic government will operate effectively. Freedom of speech, press, and assembly will exist to assure that fair and free elections may occur.

Mere outward evidence of democratic-type factors in the formal constitutional system does not always indicate that working democracy is an operational reality in a country's politics. We must look behind the façade to determine just how deeply rooted such factors are in the general pattern of political action. Most modern constitutions, including that of Mexico, establish the external forms of responsible and representative government, but only as these forms are implemented by institutionalized patterns of action do they take on real meaning. In fact, as in the case of Mexico, the most meaningful democratic institutions sometimes operate almost completely outside of the formal constitutional agencies.

Because of the essentially interactive nature of the social, economic, and political forces which go to make up a democratic syndrome, any attempt to legislate democracy as a political end in itself appears foredoomed to failure. The several factors involved must evolve together so as to provide a balanced pattern which can act as a check upon extremes of every sort. Too little respect for the individual, for example, can lead to despotism in a social system, too much to anarchy. Attempts at obtaining social and political cohesiveness through enforced conformity can lead to dictatorship, just as refusal of large factions to conform to a generally accepted value system can lead ultimately to civil war. In this sense, stable democracy must result from an evolutionary process rather than from the off-the-cuff decisions of a revolutionary clique. The amount of inertia inherent in such an evolutionary process is strikingly evident in the history of the slow formation of Mexico's present political system, which is not yet completely stabilized.

Fortunately, the very interdependence of the forces which make up democracy means that once they have become institutionalized in a political system, they tend to support and build one upon the other. After all, a pattern of action becomes institutionalized because it is in harmony with the system in which it operates. If it clashes, either the action pattern proves unworkable and disappears, or the system adjusts to absorb it. Given the existence of, and the growing interaction among, forces which make for democracy, the speed with which a democratic syndrome becomes reality depends a great deal upon the intensity of influence each and all of the democratizing factors can bring upon the government process as compared with those forces which hinder limited, responsible, and popular government.

No precise formula can determine just when the democratic syndrome becomes operative in a given country's political system and makes itself manifest to the world. More than likely, once the minima of social and economic conditions have been achieved and had time to work upon the country's politics, the breakthrough comes when the majority of thinking and politically aware citizens begin to conceive of themselves as living in a democratic state and to conduct themselves accordingly. Once this happens, the individual citizen finds himself in a situation in which he reasonably can anticipate that his legitimate day-to-day needs and desires — social, economic, and political — are limited only by the wealth of the country and his own ability is satisfy them. Despite a carry-over of some antidemocratic practices, most of the major patterns of life in the democratic system will complement each other, for the very concept of system implies continuity as well as adjustment among the activities of persons.

DEMOCRACY IN MEXICO

As suggested above, the Mexicans have not yet accomplished a complete syndrome of democracy, even in terms of their own culture and value system. Just before the 1958 election, one Mexican observer wrote that ". . . we have democracy 364 days a year and lack it only on one — election day." This statement overstates the case, both for democracy during the year and against it on election day, for within our definition of the term a political system cannot be democratic most of the year, only to reverse itself on election day. But this does not mean that the pattern of symptoms which could combine to produce a democratic syndrome in Mexico is not well advanced. On the contrary, in spite of the negative forces which continue to impede the evolution of a complete working democracy for Mexico at this time the development of conditions favoring the concept is advancing rapidly.

Examples of the factors hindering democratic government have appeared throughout this book. We know, for example, that Mexico's political system still does not rest upon a sufficiently broad base of nationally oriented, economically secure, and politically aware citizens either to assure representation of every legitimate interest in the deciding of public policy or to produce in certain of those who govern a fully developed sense of political responsibility to every individual, regardless of status or position. We know, too, that strategically located functional interest associations such as the government bureaucrats union or certain other labor groups enjoy unusually advantageous positions in the political process, and that these and other associations often are manipulated by their leaders for personal benefit, even at the expense of the rank-and-file members. We know that neither the internal nominating procedures of the official party nor the elections themselves are entirely free of per-

nicious influences intruding themselves for the personal benefit of certain politicians. We know, finally, that in the political process the individual unaffiliated with some formally organized interest association, be it inside or out of the PRI, finds it very difficult to make his voice heard, and that this condition probably will endure so long as the broad mass of Mexicans lack any strong sense of political initiative because of inadequate education, economic insecurity, or an incomplete feeling of participation in the nation.

On the social and economic level, as opposed to the political, even those citizens who have adjusted successfully to the conditions inherent in Western life do not have deeply ingrained in their consciousness and in all of their habit patterns that solid core of shared values and respect for the other individual per se that seems so important an ingredient in the formation of a democratic syndrome. Only too clearly, the benefits of industrialization, of easy communication, of Westernization in the material sense, have not spread out evenly throughout the country. Until quite recently, the urban areas have taken the lion's share, and even this portion flowed principally into the pockets of a relatively small middle and upper class. The very reform clauses of the Constitution of 1917, of which the Mexicans are so proud, have been subverted to this end at times, for they contain lists of material rights for certain groups of individuals. Although the economy of the country has not been able to satisfy all of these stated rights, the constitutional promises not only tempted but seemingly encouraged those individuals or interest groups which were stronger or better organized to bring pressure upon government, demanding their "legal rights," perhaps at the expense of the less competitive, who sometimes were pushed below the subsistence level, or even at the expense of the development of the country as a whole. In spite of all of the advanced social legislation contained in the constitution, this sudden-death kind of "collective

Social Darwinism" too often has been the practice in Mexico.

Without for a moment ignoring the negative factors mentioned here and elaborated throughout this study, it appears to me that opposing, positive factors favoring responsible, representative, and limited government are in the ascendancy in Mexico today. In time they should grow in strength, each complementing the other, until at last they join together to provide the country with an operating democratic syndrome based upon its own culture and values.

In fact, the evolutionary process already is well advanced, for side by side with the negative factors noted in the earlier chapters of this book is evidence of a great deal of positive accomplishment in the struggle to establish working democracy in Mexico. As the operations of the political decision-making process become more institutionalized, an effective constitutional system has evolved, even though it does not always follow identically the letter of the law laid down in 1917. Despite obvious weaknesses in this governing system, it does seem to take into account all of the principal and most active interest groups and associations when the highest public officers are being selected and when major policy questions are decided. Moreover, the political system is flexible enough to permit access of new groups and associations representing developing interests which grow out of changes in the social and economic environment.

More important still, from the point of view of the individual, changes in the Mexican environment are both speeding up and proliferating at an almost geometric rate, as Westernization reaches out with roads and radios and schools to embrace all of the Mexicans in a single national life. Not only are the vast majority of Mexicans being exposed to new ideas and the possibility of material change, but the value system within which they operate is being affected by these new concepts. More important in this context is the way in which, as Westernization turns more and more

Mexicans into nationally aware and politically conscious citizens, the medium through which it occurs — the Revolution of 1910 — has become identified with the values of democratic government.

To date, the propaganda line of the revolutionary governments, that Mexicans live in a democratic environment, has not been fully implemented because, as suggested in Chapter IV, the dilemma of the Revolution was that it had to set about providing suitable social and economic conditions before the political goals of democratic government could be achieved. Now that new and more suitable conditions do exist, the minds of many Mexicans are ready to absorb new understandings of the role of the individual in society and of his responsibilities to his fellow man. The seeds of these ideas have been planted in minds already open to change, so that they can take root and bear fruit in the form of socialized action later. In the Mexican world of violently conflicting values, the most consistent and dynamic force of the past half-century has been the Revolution, which does equate with an urge toward democracy, no matter how differently each Mexican may understand the meaning of that word. The social myth can have profound influence over the political activities of men; for Mexico, the myth of democracy, believed by and acted upon by enough citizens, could provide the final tie to bind together the increasingly strong democratic influences into an operative democratic syndrome.

No one who knows Mexico would argue that the country already has attained a working democratic system, or that it is the most democratic country in Latin America today, though one might well argue that in the fifty years since the outbreak of the Revolution more has been done there to solve the real problems hindering development of such a system than in any of the other republics of the area. Political scientists who specialize in Latin American politics tend to rate Mexico rather high in democratic traits, particularly in compari-

son with the other "Indian" countries of
Latin America which face similar social
and cultural problems. . . .

DEMOCRACY UNDER PRESIDENT
LÓPEZ MATEOS

During the interregnum period between
the nomination of Adolfo López Mateos
and his formal inauguration on December
1, 1958, and even during the first period of
his administration, scattered but impressive
evidence appeared to suggest that some of
the democratic concepts which have taken
root in Mexican soil are beginning to
sprout. Despite the somewhat disappoint-
ing turnout of voters, due to the absence of
qualified opposition, the presidential campaign itself indicated that a higher proportion of thinking Mexicans have begun to
concern themselves about politics, not with
the old goal of immediate and personal
aggrandizement but with the understanding that honest, effective, and responsible
government is a worthy goal in itself, one
that could pay them valuable dividends in
the long run, no matter what their means
of livelihood or role in life may be.

New political attitudes were not limited
to essentially passive intellectualizing, however, for hitherto quiescent interest groups
throughout the country took advantage of
the relaxed election and presidential transfer period to press home demands for particular interests which the leaders of the
interest associations nominally representing
them had failed to win. Some of these
movements already have been mentioned.
The attempts of leftist, anti-BUO leaders
to capture control of the labor unions representing railroaders, oil workers, electrical
workers, and primary-school teachers in the
Federal District, among others, using real
and fancied grievances as a lever, and the
consequent efforts of the established CTM
and other BUO leadership to protect their
positions by initiating their own threat of
a general strike to win wage increases for
their followers are a case in point. So are
the attempts, again led by leftists, of large
numbers of landless *peones* to obtain their

own farms by invading already cultivated
lands held by others, particularly in the
northwestern states of Sinaloa, Sonora, and
Baja California. In the context of this
study, it matters less that these movements
were led by leftists than that these leaders
were able to find persons among formally
apolitical and passive portions of the citizenry who were willing to take action on
their own behalf, indicating a growing
popular initiative that had lain dormant
since the violent days of the Revolution of
1910.

This same growth of popular initiative
manifested itself in broader political terms
at the state and local level of government
during this same period. In at least two
states, San Luis Potosí and Zacatecas, late
1958 and early 1959 saw a general cross-
section of the citizens uniting in attempts
to oust long-entrenched state political
bosses. In both cases the struggle centered
in attempts of the state *cacique*[2] to impose
his hand-picked candidates in *municipio*
elections and, unlike previous disturbances
at this level, such as that at León in 1945,
the popular reaction was widespread and
cut across party lines. Social development
had at long last reached a level at which
the general citizenry no longer was willing
to tolerate the type of strong-man government that has continued to control some
of the local units long past the evolution
of more responsible authority at the national level. In the case of San Luis Potosí,
at least, the governor was forced out in
favor of a more popular person.

President López Mateos himself demonstrated, both in his reaction to the above
incidents and in his general administrative
program, that he recognizes and encourages the expansion of popular participation
in government affairs and the activities of
the revolutionary party. Among his first
official acts in the presidential office was a
general amnesty freeing student leaders
who had been involved in incidents at the
Polytechnical Institute and the National

---

[2] Political "boss." [Editor's note.]

University, together with anti-BUO labor leaders who had precipitated the series of strikes which marked the transfer of presidential power, and radical farm leaders who had led the landless *paracaidistas* in their invasion of farm lands. As his predecessor had done in controlling the extreme wings of the revolutionary party before 1959, however, so President López Mateos made it very clear that his acts of conciliation in no way indicated abrogation of presidential power. To demonstrate that in a democratic system rights carry with them a corollary responsibility, the new chief executive did not hesitate to resort to force in the face of irresponsible or illegal acts upon the part of popular leaders, if the occasion demanded force. . . .

If President López Mateos' reaction to the pressures brought upon his administration by specific emerging interests indicates a readiness to allow them access to and participation in the decision-making process, his general program went far beyond reacting to pressures brought upon him. It encouraged the kinds of governmental and private activity which would speed up and expand preparation of Mexico's masses for popular participation in public affairs and politics. During his first year in office, expenditures for education made up the largest single budget item, and his Education Minister, Sr. Jaime Torres Bodet, inaugurated a crash program for a drastic increase in numbers of schools and teachers and, very important, for a strong improvement in their quality. Carrying out his campaign promise, President López Mateos sought to use government spending policies to encourage the geographic diversification of industry away from Mexico City and into the hinterland. He also tried to make more money available for government development projects in the nonurban areas of the country — first by attempting to operate the government petroleum monopoly on a more businesslike basis, cutting back labor featherbedding, and raising the retail price of petroleum products out of the subsidy class to allow a small profit for reinvest-

ment by the government; next by removing the government's small business loan agency, *Nacional Financiera,* from control over some of the more successful businesses it had financed, through sale of its stock holdings to the public; and finally by easing the drain on the national treasury that poor management and inefficient labor on the nationalized railways had forced.

All of these activities suggest that President López Mateos not only sought to extend as many as possible of the benefits of the Revolution to the broad mass of population but that he was both prepared and strong enough to do so in the face of the opposition of long-entrenched labor and business groups which had enjoyed a favored position in their economic and political roles. He strengthened the popular feeling that his administration would attempt to serve the interests of every Mexican who was sufficiently aware and politically active enough to participate in politics by insisting that General Alfonso Corona del Rosal, who was appointed new president of the central committee of the PRI, institute a reorganization of the party's internal operations on much more democratic lines, including the slight liberalizing of *municipio* nominating procedures mentioned above. López Mateos even went so far as to encourage the two chambers of Congress to assume a slightly stronger role in discussing policy before them for passage. In fact, certain fairly important provisions of the president's bill reorganizing portions of the executive departments were amended in the Chamber of Deputies and these amendments were upheld by the Senate, so that they became part of the law.

Quite clearly, the rapidly growing number of examples of mass interest about, pressure upon, and participation in, politics, government, and the decision-making process cannot be divorced from the equally compelling increased evidence of presidential policy during both the Ruiz Cortines and the López Mateos administrations of opening the political system to any and every Mexican who becomes sufficiently aware to demand entry to this process. In this sense, the ever-growing forces for democratic government, which well up from the general citizenry as social and economic conditions prepare them for an effective role in the political process, are being supplemented and encouraged by the chief executives who have won nomination to their high office precisely because they represent in their views and their past careers those same forces which make for representative, responsible, and limited government.

SUGGESTIONS FOR ADDITIONAL READING

The literature in English on the various aspects of the Mexican Revolution tends to be generally sympathetic to the hopes and aspirations continuously expressed by the revolutionary spokesmen, even though specific policies or actions may be subjected to harsh criticism. In those areas of revolutionary activity intimately touching the interests of the United States or its citizens, however, a good deal of polemical literature attacking the revolution's fundamental assumptions can be found; the Church-State issue and the oil problem particularly engendered great heat and stimulated many publications.

The revolution must be considered in terms of conditions existing in 1910, but unfortunately the Díaz period has attracted little serious scholarship on the part of U.S. writers. Wilfred H. Callcott, *Liberalism in Mexico* (Stanford: Stanford University Press, 1931) is an old stand-by, sound but incomplete, and Ernest Gruening, *Mexico and Its Heritage* (New York: Century Co., 1928) presents a doleful picture of the social and economic, as well as the political, conditions prior to 1910. The only biography of Díaz even approaching objectivity is Carleton Beals, *Porfirio Diaz: Dictator of Mexico* (Philadelphia: Lippincott, 1932), but his general evaluation is a bit too negative. James Creelman, whose famous 1908 interview with Díaz did much to stimulate the Madero revolution of 1910, presented the best of the contemporary eulogistic accounts in *Diaz, Master of Mexico* (New York: D. Appleton and Company, 1911). John Kenneth Turner, *Barbarous Mexico* (Chicago: C. H. Kerr and Co., 1911), and Henry Baerlein, *Mexico, the Land of Unrest: Being Chiefly an Account of What Produced the Outbreak of 1910* (London: Herbert and Daniel, 1913), found nothing attractive about the Díaz regime while Edward I. Bell, *The Political Shame of Mexico* (New York: McBride,

Nast and Company, 1914) castigated the mentality which gave support to Díaz and was responsible for Madero's overthrow and death. In addition to these works, many of the titles mentioned below also contain chapters on various aspects of the Díaz period.

The most convenient source for a general picture of developments since 1910 may be found in Howard Cline's two books originally issued as hard-backs but now in paper: *The United States and Mexico* (New York: Atheneum, 1963), a revised and enlarged edition of an earlier (1953) Harvard Press publication, emphasizes domestic rather than international affairs. *Mexico; Revolution to Evolution: 1940–1960* (New York: Oxford University Press, 1963), belies its title, however, since much of the book concerns the period prior to 1940. Frank Tannenbaum, *Peace by Revolution* (New York: Columbia University Press, 1933) gives a highly enthusiastic account of the progress to date of publication and should be read in conjunction with his more nostalgic *Mexico: The Struggle for Peace and Bread* (New York: Alfred A. Knopf, 1951). Tomme Clark Call, *The Mexican Venture; From Political to Industrial Revolution in Mexico* (New York: Oxford University Press, 1953) and John W. F. Dulles, *Yesterday in Mexico: A Chronicle of the Revolution, 1919–1936* (Austin: The University of Texas Press, 1961) both have excellent material, although Dulles is somewhat uncritical in his judgments and selections. Arthur P. Whitaker (ed.) *Mexico Today: A General Picture of the Objectives and Achievements of our Southern Neighbor* (Annals of the American Academy of Political and Social Science, Vol. 208, 1940) consists of a series of articles of varying degrees of excellence. Frank Brandenburg, *The Making of Modern Mexico* (Englewood Cliffs, N. J.: Prentice-Hall, Inc.,

1964), emphasizes the period since 1940.

Three scholarly books deal with the early phases of the revolution. Charles C. Cumberland, *Mexican Revolution: Genesis Under Madero* (Austin: The University of Texas Press, 1952) and Stanley R. Ross, *Francisco I. Madero: Apostle of Mexican Democracy* (New York: Columbia University Press, 1955) cover the same period in much the same way. Robert E. Quirk, *The Mexican Revolution, 1914–1915: The Convention of Aguascalientes* (Bloomington: Indiana University Press, 1960) is an excellent study of a critical period. The period from 1915 to 1925 is covered with books of dubious merit, although Gruening is fairly complete and relatively objective. Rosa King, *Tempest Over Mexico* (Boston: Little, Brown, 1935) consists of the charming observations of an English lady who lived in Cuernavaca. Less charming, and certainly less sympathetic to Zapata, is Harry H. Dunn, *The Crimson Jester: Zapata of Mexico* (New York: McBride, 1934), while Edgcumb Pinchon, *Zapata the Unconquerable* (New York: Doubleday, Doran, 1941) sees that agrarian leader in a completely favorable light. Jorge Vera Estañol, *Carranza and His Bolshevik Regime* (Los Angeles: Wayside Press, 1920) and Francis McCullagh, *Red Mexico: A Rein of Terror in America* (New York: L. Carrier and Company, 1926) agree on the general nature of the revolution, but for different reasons. Vicente Blasco Ibañez, *Mexico in Revolution* (New York: E. P. Dutton, 1920) is the Spanish novelist's reaction after having been encouraged by the government to come to Mexico. E. J. Dillon, *President Obregón, A World Reformer* (London: Hutchinston & Co., 1923) is, as the title implies, a contemporary panegyric. Lázaro Cárdenas, too, has been the object of eulogistic writing; both William Cameron Townsend, *Lázaro Cárdenas: Mexican Democrat* (Ann Arbor: G. Wahr Publishing Co., 1952) and Nathaniel and Sylvia Weyl, *Reconquest of Mexico: The Years of Lázaro Cárdenas* (New York and London: Oxford University Press, 1939) see Cárdenas as a great, beneficent force in Mexican revolutionary political and social development. J. H. Plenn, *Mexico Marches* (Indianapolis: The Bobbs-Merrill Company, 1939) concentrates on the year 1938 as a focal point from which he ranges backward in a chatty and sympathetic manner.

Something of the bitterness and the intransigency of the contending parties over the oil dispute can be found in a series of publications by the Standard Oil Company of New Jersey and by the Mexican government, all published in 1939 and 1940. Standard Oil, *Confiscation or Expropriation?* is a collection of articles or booklets published by the company in 1939–40, constituting a violent attack on the integrity of the Mexicans. A few months later the company published *Present Status of the Mexican Oil "Expropriations," 1940,* to which Mexico replied with *The True Facts About the Expropriation of the Oil Companies' Properties in Mexico* (Mexico: 1940). This in turn brought forth *The Reply to Mexico* (1940) on the part of Standard Oil. William E. McMahon, who had many years of experience in Mexico with U.S. oil companies, contributed what he claimed to be a carefully researched and accurate account in *Two Strikes and Out* (Garden City, N. Y.: Country Life Press Corp., 1939) but it was, in fact, as biased as the foregoing works. Roscoe Gaither, *Expropriation in Mexico: The Facts and the Law* (New York: William Morrow and Company, 1940) falls into the same category, but Harlow S. Person, from whose *Mexican Oil* an excerpt is included herein, gives a more balanced view. Wendell C. Gordon, *The Expropriation of Foreign-Owned Property in Mexico* (Washington: Public Affairs Press, 1941) includes the oil question in his general discussion of expropriation, which he presents with a degree of detachment. Richard J. Powell, *The Mexican Petroleum Industry, 1938–1950* (Berkeley and Los Angeles: University of California Bureau of Business and Economic Research, 1956) gives a somewhat pessimistic view of the government's operation of the industry.

The definitive work, written from a Mexican point of view but objective nonetheless, on the experiences since 1938 is Antonio Bermúdez, *The Mexican National Petroleum Industry . . . A Case Study in Nationalization* (Institute of Hispanic American and Luso-Brazilian Studies, Stanford University, 1963). Bermúdez was the Director General of the government company, Petroleos Mexicanos, for twelve critical years; the book contains a great deal of valuable statistical data.

No serious scholar has attempted a full-scale study of the Church-State conflict, although the relevant chapters in John Lloyd Mecham, *Church and State in Latin America* (Chapel Hill: University of North Carolina Press, 1934) gives an excellent juridico-legal account to the date of publication. Graham Greene, *Another Mexico* (New York: The Viking Press, 1939) published in England under the title of *The Lawless Roads* (London: Eyre and Spottiswoode, 1950), roundly condemns the government for what Mr. Greene considered the reign of terror of the 'twenties. Joseph Schlarman, *Mexico: The Land of Volcanoes* (Milwaukee: Bruce Publishing Company, 1950) and James Magner, *Men of Mexico* (Milwaukee: Bruce Publishing Company, 1943) give versions highly sympathetic to the Church. But the most scurrilous attacks on the government, and the least authenticated, come from Bishop Francis Clement Kelley of Chicago; the titles suggest the manner in which the subject is treated: *The Book of the Red and the Yellow; Being a Story of Blood and a Yellow Streak* (Chicago: The Catholic Church Extension Society of the United States of America, 1915) and *Blood-Drenched Altars: Mexican Study and Comment* (Milwaukee: Bruce Publishing Co., 1935). Emilio Portes Gil, *The Conflict Between the Civil Power and the Clergy: Historical and Legal Essay* (Mexico: Press of the Ministry of Foreign Affairs, 1935) is a strong indictment of the clerical posi-

tion, written by an ex-president then functioning as the attorney-general. Ernest Galarza, *The Roman Catholic Church as a Factor in the Political and Social History of Mexico* (Sacramento, Calif.: The Capital Press, 1928) is perhaps even more condemnatory. All of these books were written at the height of the quarrel and do not reflect the *modus vivendi* which has been obtained since about 1940.

The best works on the agrarian reform program in English are, unfortunately, badly out of date. Frank Tannenbaum, *The Mexican Agrarian Revolution* (New York: The Macmillan Company, 1929) gives a good picture of the background and the legal status to the date of publication, but at that point the program had barely begun. Eyler N. Simpson, *The Ejido: Mexico's Way Out* (Chapel Hill: University of North Carolina Press, 1937) is a magnificent book, but written before the Cárdenas push. Nathan L. Whetten, *Rural Mexico* (Chicago: Univ. of Chicago Press, 1948) is an excellent study, but principally based upon data collected in the 1940 census. George M. McBride, *Land Systems of Mexico* (New York: American Geographical Society, 1923) is an outstanding work by a competent geographer, stressing the nineteenth century. Koka Freier and Henrik Enfield, *People in Ejidos* (New York: F. A. Praeger, 1954) gives a rather idealistic view of the life on the ejidos.

The best single volume on the economic structure and potential is Combined Mexican Working Party, *Economic Development in Mexico* (Baltimore: Johns Hopkins Press, 1953) one of the series of country studies done under the auspices of the International Bank of Reconstruction and Development. As is true of all this series, it is detached and objective, filled with data, and fairly dull reading. Call's *The Mexican Venture*, mentioned earlier, is primarily concerned with the intervention of the state into the economic process. Nacional Financiera, *The Economic Development of Mexico During a Quarter of a Century* (Mexico: Nacional Financiera,

1959) is an optimistic view presented by one of Mexico's governmental development agencies. Marjorie Ruth Clark, *Organized Labor in Mexico* (Chapel Hill: University of North Carolina Press, 1934) and W. E. Moore, *Industrialization and Labor* (Ithaca: Cornell University Press, 1951) provide adequate coverage for the period and the subject matter treated, but combined they do not give a complete analysis of the labor situation. Some of the fiscal problems created by the early phases of the revolution may be found in Walter F. Mc-Caleb, *Present and Past Banking in Mexico* (New York: Harper and Brothers, 1920), Edwin Walter Kemmerer, *Inflation and Revolution: Mexico's Experience, 1912–1917* (Princeton: Princeton University Press, 1940), and Edgar Turlington, *Mexico and Her Foreign Creditors* (New York: Columbia University Press, 1930); in both McCaleb and Turlington the revolution is merely an incidental part of a larger historical study.

Mexican revolutionary education has attracted a great deal of attention primarily because of the extremely low literacy rate in 1910, the relationship of the educational question to that of Church-State relations, and the experimentation in which the government has been engaged. But in recent years experimentation has been lessened — or at least is undramatic — and the Church-State conflict is no longer a burning issue, so most of the books dealing with the subject are dated. Both George C. Booth, *Mexico's School-Made Society* (Stanford: Stanford University Press, 1941) and George I. Sanchez, *Mexico: A Revolution by Education* (New York: Viking Press, 1936) discuss the Church-State issue, and both take the Church to task for its educational failure. George F. Kneller, *The Education of the Mexican Nation* (New York: Columbia University Press, 1951) is a concise work which includes all aspects until about 1948, and Marjorie C. Johnston, *Education in Mexico* (Washington: U.S. Department of Health, Education and Welfare, Office of Education, 1956) is an even shorter summary which contains later data. George I. Sanchez, *The Development of Higher Education in Mexico* (New York: Columbia University Press, 1944) and Irma Wilson, *Mexico: A Century of Educational Thought* (New York: Hispanic Institute in the United States, 1941) are chiefly historical.

Robert Scott, *Mexican Government in Transition,* from which a selection is taken, is by all odds the best work in English on Mexican political development, although those portions on politics of the previously-mentioned Brandenburg book merit close reading. William P. Tucker, *The Mexican Government Today* (Minneapolis: University of Minnesota Press, 1957) is an excellent description of the governmental institutions, but by its nature was obsolescent at the time it was published. John J. Johnson, *Political Change in Latin America* (Stanford: Stanford University Press, 1958) and Edwin Lieuwen, *Arms and Politics in Latin America* (New York: Council on Foreign Relations, 1960) contain excellent sections on the emerging middle class and the decline of militarism, respectively. Karl M. Schmitt, *Communism in Mexico* (Austin: The University of Texas Press, 1965) is a detailed study of the failure of communism to make real headway there.

For those students who wish to go beyond the material listed here, the most convenient guide for works in English appears in R. A. Humphreys, *Latin American History: A Guide to the Literature in English* (London and New York: Oxford University Press, 1958). A limited guide which includes titles in Spanish as well may be found in American Universities Field Staff, *A Selective Bibliography: Asia, Africa, Eastern Europe, Latin America* (New York: 1960). But the essential guide is the annual *Handbook of Latin American Studies,* which began publication in 1936 at Harvard and continued in later years at the University of Florida.